BOXING

BOXING
THE CHAMPIONS

BY KEN JONES AND CHRIS SMITH

This edition published 1992
by the Promotional Reprint
Company Limited for
Bookmart Limited, Desford Road,
Enderby, Leicester, UK

Designed by Graeme Murdoch

Produced by Mandarin Offset
Printed in Hong Kong

ISBN 1 85648 052 6

PICTURE ACKNOWLEDGEMENTS:

AP: 32, 36, 39 (both pictures), 45, 47, 53, 57, 59 (both pictures), 61 (bottom), 81, 85, 89, 91, 105, 106, 123, 139, 142, 145, 153, 161, 163, 167, 175 (right), 219, 220.

UPI: 12, 15, 151.

Popperfoto: 29, 61 (top), 63, 140.

Thomson Newspapers: 155

The Independent: 203.

Press Association: 218.

CONTENTS

'In the clearing stood a boxer,
a fighter by his trade . . .'
Paul Simon

The authors are grateful for the assistance
of *The Sunday Mirror*, *The Independent*,
Observer and *The Sunday Times* in
the preparation of this book.

INTRODUCTION

Sometimes I go back to the town where I was born and, if nothing urgent springs to mind, I leave the motorway at Newport and drive up to Abergavenny, then westward through Brynmawr and Tredegar so that Merthyr Tydfil can be reached from the brow at Dowlais top. The town lies below you there and at a distance you are seeing it much as it was observed by travellers a century or more ago.

From that elevation you can look out across the valley and imagine what Merthyr was like before the onset of a terrible depression: the searing blast of insatiable furnaces; the ceaseless cascading spew of molten waste cooling to form sullen escarpments on the hillsides; bleak ridges of grey-black slurry brooding over the landscape; withering hardship – the Devil's place Merthyr was.

Quiet now; land reclaimed, the valley collieries but forgotten catacombs; Plymouth, Cwm and Castle Pit, where my father toiled when just a boy of 14, rising before dawn and not seeing daylight for months on end; the great foundries of Dowlais and Cyfartha laid to waste; the forbidding ironmasters and coal owners long since in their graves.

But towards the middle of the nineteenth century, a small community with no significant history was transformed into an industrial hell-hole, its name to be known around the world: a bawdy, brawling Klondike, attracting both the rural Welsh and swarms of immigrant workers – English, Irish, Italians, Spaniards – many to endure conditions of indescribable squalor: infant mortality of such devastating proportions that a child was lucky to survive five years.

Thousands settled along the infested banks of the River Taff and the Glamorgan Canal that carried iron down to the sea at Cardiff; exploited, corrupted, amoral, condemned to a miserable existence in

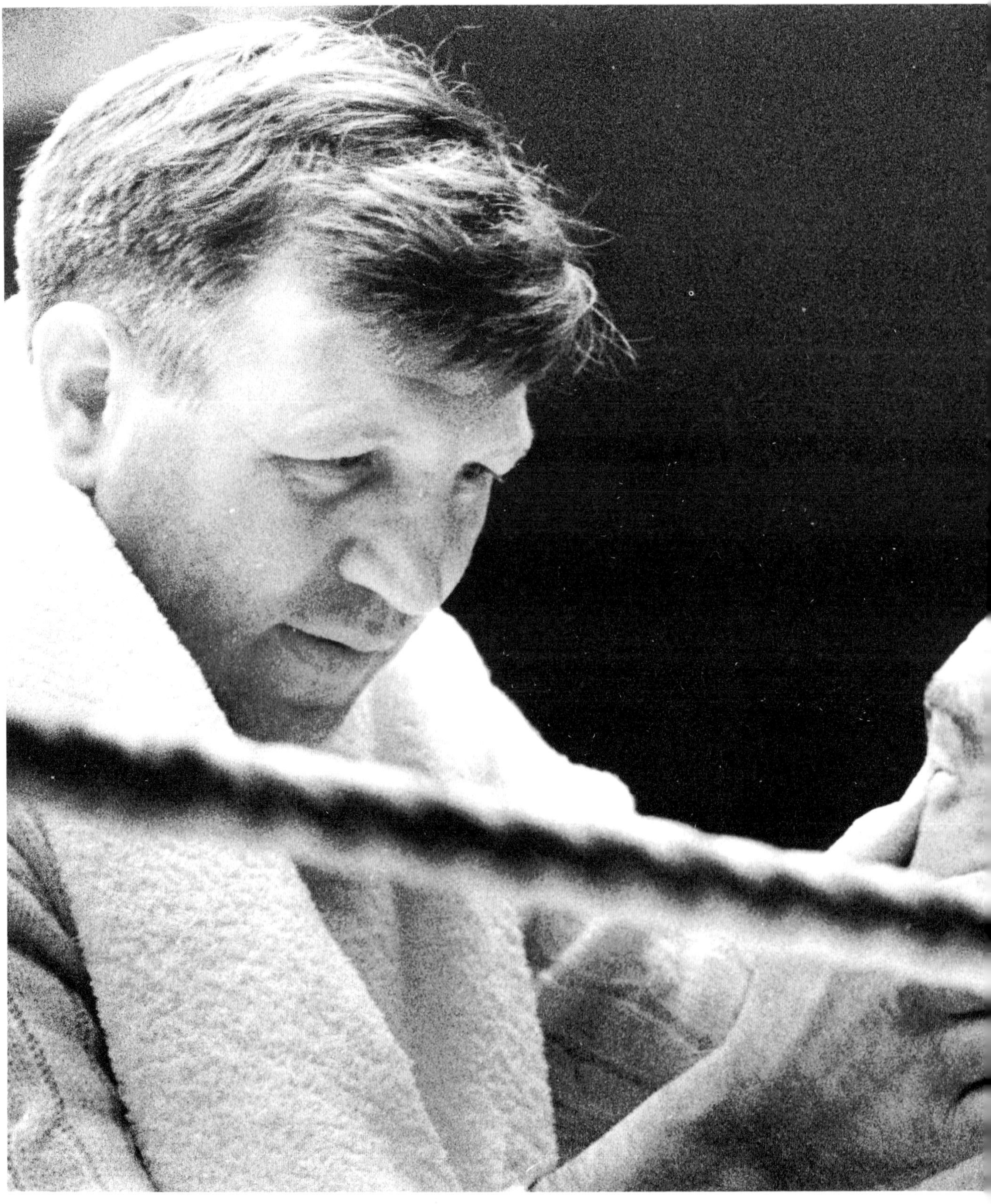

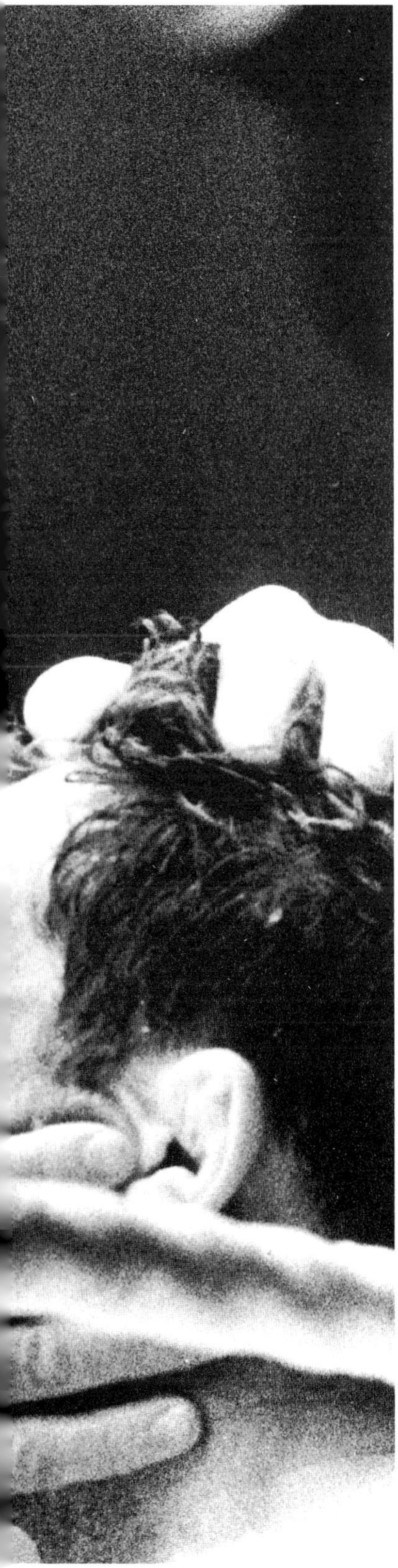

Eddie Thomas, at work with Howard Winstone, employs the skill that gained him a reputation as one of the best corner men in the business.

cheap lodging-houses and in a shanty town of such pervading awfulness that the district of Georgetown around the Iron Bridge (notorious 'China') evoked a sense of everlasting doom.

It is no exaggeration to suggest that Merthyr once qualified as one of the hardest towns on earth, its riverside ghettoes the natural habitat of murderers, tricksters, shysters, thieves, prostitutes and footpads.

In that grim setting, fist-fights were a way of life. Self-appointed champions emerged, taking on all comers, most notably Shoni Ysgubor Fawr, a brooding figure of unassailable legend who drew vast crowds and was thought to be supreme throughout Wales.

When I first heard tell of him, refracted images flourished in my mind. I could see Fawr striding out through the clamorous assembly, huge and red-haired, seconds scurrying at his side, the epitome of a noble warrior, if in truth a villain who ruled briefly as 'Emperor of the Taff bridges'.

Not so long ago, I was persuaded to attend a contest staged in Merthyr by my friend Eddie Thomas, the former British and European welterweight champion who, as fighter, manager and philanthropic promoter, has been going in with hard men for more than 40 years. He had brought together Martin Galleozzie and Johnny Wall for the lightweight championship of Wales and predicted it would be a 'tidy scrap'. From what I remember of the occasion, both men were paid £1,000 but the unavoidable impression was that they would have fought in the street outside for nothing and probably not without assistance, because the families showed up in force and a word out of place might have enabled Thomas to dispense with the undercard.

The fight proceeded more or less as Thomas predicted; a tidy set-to indeed, not of the highest order, but nonetheless thrilling and a reminder that it was once difficult to find anybody in Merthyr whose grandparents had all been born there. The Galleozzies were obviously of Italian descent and the Walls can probably be traced to the north-east of England. Now they represented districts at the opposite ends of a Welsh town and from their accents it would have been extremely unwise to suggest otherwise.

A fighting man and his memories. Howard Winstone, the Welshman from Merthyr Tydfil, who defeated Mitsundri Seki to become Featherweight Champion of the World after losing three times to the late Vicente Saldivar of Mexico.

Ethnic influences may explain a lot about Merthyr's contribution to the annals of Welsh sport. Rugby football, the national game, failed to take hold there but a stream of outstandingly talented soccer players emerged between the two Great Wars, among them Bryn Jones, one of my father's four brothers, who figured in a world record transfer of £14,000 when Arsenal signed him from Wolverhampton Wanderers in 1938.

Of course, pugilism is embedded in the Merthyr psyche – an instinct Eddie Thomas attributes to the harsh experiences endured by past generations. One of the many Merthyr legends speaks of children coming so angrily into the world that their fists were already clenched. There are many others and all colourfully drawn, as my friend Hugh McIlvanney of the *Observer* discovered in 1965 when researching a feature about Howard Winstone, one of the town's modern heroes:

> If Howard Winstone beats Vicente Saldivar of Mexico and takes the featherweight championship of the world at Earls Court on 7 September the people of Merthyr will see it as merely the fulfilment of the natural law. They are already infectiously convinced that Merthyr is in possession of some kind of cosmic championship, that the town and its sons have established firsts or bests in all the significant fields of human endeavour. When Eddie Thomas, Winstone's manager, reminds you that Britain's first coal was dug out from the Merthyr hillsides and that the town was once 'the

EVERLAST

No heavyweight this century has represented British boxing more nobly than Tommy Farr, the Welshman from Tonypandy who went 15 rounds with Joe Louis in 1937.

industrial capital of the world' he is simply introducing you to a mounting scale of claimed distinctions which ends in bizarre magnificence. 'First man Albert Pierrepoint hung threw a woman down the coke ovens over there.'

Eddie Thomas lives in an imposing Victorian house set up on the right as you come down from Dowlais through Penydarren towards the top of the town, and just above where the rink stood. Many famous Welsh fighters appeared there and at Wonderland, Snow's Pavilion, the Labour Club and the Drill Hall and Thomas is not inclined to go easy with the superlatives when addressing their memory. 'They all came and showed Merthyr their hands,' he said one bitterly cold day after we had trudged up to a plateau of slag, beyond the row of miners' cottages where he was born. 'Jimmy Wilde, Freddie Welsh, Jim Driscoll, some of the greatest fighters the world has ever seen. Tommy Farr would bet himself with half-crowns on the apron of the ring. No amateurs here then, it was always for money. Different now, life has changed and most of the old traditions have faded away. But I still sense there are kids who want to fight, although it is hard to imagine Merthyr will ever again produce anyone as gifted as Howard Winstone or as determined as poor Johnny Owen.'

Owen never recovered from a coma after being knocked out when challenging Lupe Pintor of Mexico for the world bantamweight championship on 19 September 1980. Although Thomas had played no part in the Welshman's career, he could not avoid calling the old game into question. 'I had to ask myself whether it was worth going on. But boxing is in me as it was in him. That isn't easy to explain because there is more to it than money or fame or even the knowledge that people who follow boxing are living out a part of their lives through you. There is an

Although only 23, Farr had been in more than 200 professional contests when he challenged Joe Louis for the championship. . . . Louis won comfortably on pointss but Farr, tough and stubborn, confused the champion with a style shaped in the boxing booths of his youth (he fought his first 10-rounder a fortnight after his thirteenth birthday) and gave an heroic performance.

instinct deep inside and it keeps leading you back to the ring.'

Despite constant problems with his weight, Thomas was the 10 st 7 lb champion of Great Britain, Europe and the Empire and was considered good enough to be a contender for the world title, then held by Sugar Ray Robinson. He went on to form a productive alliance with Ken Buchanan of Scotland, taking him to the world lightweight title, and with Winstone, the featherweight champion, who fully restored Merthyr's reputation as a fighting town.

When at work in the ring, skilful and spirited, Winstone evoked images of old hill scrappers, but there is plenty of Merthyr history in his blood – Welsh, English, Irish, Jewish. I see him now and again at lunches and dinners.

'How are things Howard?'

'All right see.' The voice pitched high and primed for wickedness.

It is hard to believe he is 50 and that 25 years have slipped away since his three great tussles with the late Vicente Saldivar.

Because the fundamental objective in boxing is to induce a state of mind known commonly as unconsciousness, people who think it to be an abomination, and therefore a blight on society, may find it difficult to believe that Winstone and Saldivar became friends.

A passion for the sport is no easier to explain. Maybe I should respond more readily to the ambivalence that refuses to be denied whenever there is a tragedy like the one which overtook Johnny Owen or a moment that emphasizes how much the game takes from so many of them.

Maybe. Maybe I should not take the road back to Merthyr and forget being lifted from my bed in the early hours when Tommy Farr went in with Joe Louis for the heavyweight championship of the world.

Many, many years later, I sat with Farr at his home in Hove, not long after Joe Bugner had revealed himself to be a notable pacifist when going 15 rounds with Muhammad Ali. Farr, weighing only a few pounds more than when he fought Louis, rose and then slipped easily into a crouch that was born long ago in a fairground booth and right away there was a naturalness you could never have found in Bugner. 'It's as simple as this you see,' he said. By turning his left foot outwards from the heel, he could reach six inches further forward with his left fist.

The fundamentals had not changed and the years slipped away. He remained devastatingly alert, devoutly Welsh and the past was far from being a blurr. 'I was still a young man when I met Louis, but by then I'd had almost two hundred fights. I didn't need advice. But I always remembered what they told us in the booths when we were boxing for fifteen shillings a day. If they want to fight, you box them. If they want to box, you fight them.'

When Farr recalled the Louis fight, it was more the aftermath than the happening. 'I put everything into those fifteen rounds,' he said. 'The lot. My face looked like a dug-up road. The next day my manager Ted Broadribb came to the room and said it was time we went and collected our money. I threw a telephone directory at him.'

There are other times and other places . . .

There was no beginning in that I did not set out to write about sport or ever imagine being at the ringside in New York and Las Vegas and all those other locations.

Life can be like that: you take off in one direction, a destination clear in your mind, only to be diverted somewhere else. In September 1958, a conspicuously modest career in football foreshortened by a serious injury, credulous, untrained and more than just slightly bewildered, I found myself working for the *Daily Mirror*.

In those days the *Mirror* was unquestionably a remarkable newspaper and people who say it set the highest standards ever achieved in popular journalism remember it being brash but never scurrilous or vindictive and always mindful of the truth.

From this lofty platform Peter Wilson cast a stern eye over sport, his enormous ego nourished by privilege and exaggerated projection. He was 'The World's No 1 Sports Writer' and 'The Man They Can't Gag'. As a humble gatherer of information about football, I thought those titles to be slightly ridiculous, but it soon became clear that people in sport believed Wilson to be a man of wise and independent virtue and there was no doubt that he wielded considerable influence in boxing.

In time, I was sent to assist him at the ringside. This did not amount to very much but it meant that I no longer had to settle for a cheap seat way back in the hall and could get closer to fighters, understanding them better.

Wilson used an old typewriter and carried it in a case ostentatiously festooned with labels that told of much travelling and momentous events. His eyes never strayed from the action. Significant punches and crucial manoeuvres were faithfully recorded on the typewriter and as the phrases leaped from the keyboard, I spoke them into a telephone. He employed vivid similies. A concussed boxer's eyes were 'like the windows of an empty house', an open mouth 'a pink cavern of fatigue', and because they were repeated at discreet intervals, I tried to anticipate them.

At the end of a fight I was expected to make for the dressing-rooms and return with any relevant information, although Wilson seldom allowed this to impose upon his assessment. He would then draw all the elements together and compose a more considered account, carefully chosen phrases and unequivocal judgements falling neatly into place.

On their way to the exits, passers-by would acknowledge Wilson and sometimes ask for his autograph. They did so respectfully because he gave the impression of having never been younger than middle-aged, as though preferring not to be associated with anything that might be thought frivolous. A tall, heavily built man with a distinctive moustache, he moved at a measured pace and always carried a silver-topped cane.

Of course, he was a rich source of anecdote and an autobiography published in 1977 would have been better for more of that and less of the vanity. Before the Second World War, when only in his twenties, he had covered championship fights in the United States for what was then the *Sunday Pictorial* and could speak of experiences shared with some of the most famous people in sport.

Wilson's first love was tennis and I found it difficult to reconcile his deep affection for that game's snooty traditions with a response to prize-fighting, and yet he was as much at home in sleazy gymnasiums as in the Royal Box at Wimbledon.

When expressing despair with what he observed to be the nature of modern boxing, the late Bill Daly, an American manager whose activities were once of great interest to the FBI, was once heard to declare: 'There was a time when you settled an argument by rolling a Molotov cocktail up the guy's garden path, now it's lawyers, lawyers, lawyers.'

Wilson, could hardly endorse an old reprobate's preference for the hoodlum solution but there was a night when Daly, brandishing a pearl-handled pistol, rescued the Harrovian in a New York restaurant. I found such tales fascinating and they helped to explain why boxing transferred so easily to the printed page, not merely the fighters and their immediate connections, but those who are natuarally drawn to the game: hustlers, con-men, gamblers, outright villains and small-time crooks.

If acceptance of their presence is seen to be overtly pragmatic, it ought not be taken as an endorsement of the belief that boxing is in the grip of corrupt forces – the provocative theme of Budd Schulberg's novel *The Harder They Fall.* When it was filmed, Hollywood took a liberty with Schulberg's script, betraying the instinct that inspired a work Gene Tunney, the former heavyweight champion, praised as the most authentic fiction ever written about the fight game. In the closing scene, Humphrey Bogart, playing a journalist hired to publicize El Toro Molina, an ultimately pathetic South American heavyweight victimized by mob influences, is so stricken with remorse that he types . . . Boxing Must Be Destroyed.

In fact, Schulberg was trying to protect boxing. One of the most important of modern American authors, he said his book 'exposed the deliberate exploitation of a manufactured champion, the chicanery, the greed, the casual disregard of a fighter's sensibilities and economic needs that is pugilism at its worst.'

When rumours of Muhammad Ali's diminishing responses became clinical reality, following tests in a New York hospital in September 1984, Schulberg found himself drawn once again into a worrying debate and it continues to bother him that no serious attempt has been made in the United States to establish a central controlling authority similar to the British Boxing Board of Control.

'The Greatest of all times.' Ali at the peak of his career . . .

Whatever the medical evidence, it is still not clear how much a fighter's senses are impaired by prolonged exposure to the hazards of professional boxing.

In contrast to Joe Louis and Sugar Ray Robinson, two great figures who died in bleak circumstances, Gene Tunney took full advantage of his status as heavyweight champion, becoming a successful business man and a commissioned officer in the Second World War.

His great adversary, Jack Dempsey, who ranks alongside Ali and Louis as the most emotive single fighting force this century, completed a full and contented life. Floyd Patterson, another heavyweight champion, became boxing commissioner for the State of New York.

Schulberg was confident that Ali, too, would avoid the darker experiences. 'I watched him through all those years and believed that the bad things couldn't happen. But they did. There were always the hangers on, the shysters, the freebooters, people stealing from him. He was exploited. No doubt. And yet I see no point in putting an end to boxing. That would simply send it underground to where evil flourishes.'

It was when working with, or rather for, Peter Wilson that I first sensed a shudder of ambivalence about boxing. A 12-round eliminator for the British featherweight title brought together Terry Spinks, the baby-faced East Londoner who won a gold medal at flyweight in the Melbourne Olympics of 1956, and Johnny Kidd of Scotland, a former European amateur champion.

After establishing a clear points advantage in the first half of the contest, Spinks began to wilt, taking such violent punishment that he was almost out on his feet when declared a narrow winner. Visitors were not welcome in the dressing-room but I managed to squirm through to

the corridor outside and found Spinks in a shower stall, propped against one wall, almost obscured by the steam that billowed from the hot water cascading over his slight shoulders. He asked a question, not of me but of his manager, Sammy McCarthy. 'What round is it Sammy?' he mumbled, eyes closed, not yet in full possession of his senses.

'Leave him,' McCarthy said quietly and I turned away, realizing just how much the game takes from them.

About that time, I came across Lou Josephs who, for an obvious reason, was known otherwise as One Arm Lou. Long before George Cole, in his television role of Arthur Daley, made the phrase popular, Lou had got himself some 'nice little earners' and, by employing a degree of Runyonesque charm, managed to stay out of serious trouble. He could usually be found at the smaller promotions, which were about the limit of my expectations as a boxing writer, and one night spoke of what sounded like a scam.

The scoring system then being operated in British boxing gave five points to the winner of a closely contested round and a quarter of a point less to the other man. When there was a huge difference, the marking might be 5 to 4½.

Lou hit upon the idea that as it took referees longer to scribble the lesser amount, it might be possible to discover which of two evenly matched men was ahead going into the final round, thus gaining an edge in the betting. For months he travelled the small hall circuit, studying referees through binoculars from a ringside seat. Aware of my scepticism, Lou invited me to sit with him at Shoreditch Town Hall in London, insisting he would be able to 'read' the official in charge of what was expected to be a lively featherweight contest over eight rounds. 'This one is easy,' he said. 'Middle-aged, minces [mincepies:

eyes] not too clever, holds out the card when he marks it. All I need to know is how he's got them, left and right.'

This was soon established and when the bell sounded to start the last round, it appeared that only a fraction separated the contestants. Lou was now relying upon his own judgement and with little more than a minute left, he called for the price against a draw. The referee agreed with his assessment and Lou collected beneath a sign reminding patrons that betting was prohibited.

Of course, the system was flawed. The majority of referees were not as accommodating as the man at Shoreditch and towards the end of a close contest Lou was unlikely to be laid better than even money either man.

The next time we met, he was touting tickets outside White Hart Lane, the Tottenham Hotspur Football Ground, which indicated that the system was not proving very profitable. 'Keep moving,' muttered a policeman. Lou began hopping up and down on the spot and was booked for insolence.

A year or so later, Lou telephoned the office. 'Who is this guy Ben Wright?' he growled. I was no longer working with Peter Wilson and Ben, now a successful golf commentator in the United States and by all accounts a man of some substance, had covered a fight in his absence. 'I think it's scandalous how much betting goes on at the ringside,' he said the next day.

'Always been so,' I replied.

'But there are signs declaring it illegal and nobody takes any notice.'

'So?'

'Well I'm going to write about it.'

'Please yourself.'

Ben wrote that the Board of Control should take immediate steps to ensure that the law was obeyed, hence Lou's disgruntled enquiry.

The very next week Ben was required to cover boxing again and, as there was no significant football being played that night, I went to Wembley Arena.

Ben had gone to check on the running order when Lou showed up at the ringside.

'Where is he?' he asked.

'Who?'

'You know who I mean. Ben Wright.'

'Not here tonight.'

'I know that he is.'

I told Lou to behave and he departed grumbling about some of the chaps not being very pleased. Ben had observed this going on and asked me to explain. I did so and he stiffened.

Later, as we made our way to the exit, I saw Lou standing on the stairs watching us approach.

'See you around Lou,' I said.

'Sure. And make sure Mr Wright takes care.'

Ben did not look back.

In 1969, Peter Wilson, at almost 56 years old, discovered that he had lung cancer. He fought it courageously and, after retiring to Majorca in 1972, returned annually for the Wimbledon tennis championships.

I saw him for the last time in June 1981, when Jim Watt lost the world lightweight championship to Alexis Arguello.

For more than ten years Peter had raged against the dying of the light, looking upon the real prospect of death as an affront to his dignity. After driving him into London from Wembley Arena, I felt a great sadness. We were never close but he had helped to show me the way. ■

MADISON SQUARE GARDEN

In my growing-up days, no arena was more synonymous with championship boxing than Madison Square Garden, New York. A brave attempt to revive former glories seems appropriate to a book about champions.

★ ★ ★ ★ ★

Maybe they never do come back and perhaps Madison Square Garden will never again be to boxing what it thrillingly was when the greatest of them fought there, but things are looking up on the corner of West 33rd Street and Eighth Avenue.

If they were looking down, it would surely be time for the battered old game to desert New York finally, so anyone with a genuine sense of sporting history should applaud the work being done there by Bobby Goodman, a sturdily built student of life in its most devious form.

As Goodman was once employed by Don King, the ubiquitous former numbers racketeer who continues to influence most of what goes on in the heavyweight division, it can be assumed he knows a trick or two. This, as it happens, is substantially the truth, much to the benefit of boxing at the Garden where, until recently, most of the talk was about what used to be: of Muhammad Ali and Joe Frazier; Sandy Saddler and Willie Pep; Sugar Ray Robinson, Joe Louis, Jersey Joe Walcott, and Roberto Duran. The Garden used to be in a different place. In the days of Jack Dempsey and Benny Leonard, it was 16 blocks further north; but in boxing, Mecca is where you find it and the memories linger on.

There was little more than memories left when Goodman was persuaded to take over as director of boxing and matchmaker in an attempt to restore a reputation lost to the casinos of Las Vegas and Atlantic City, where the upfront money runs to millions.

Barney Nagler, a 77-year-old veteran sportswriter who still contributes five erudite columns a week to the *Daily Racing Form*, said: 'In its great and spirited days boxing was the blood of the Garden but, with the advent of television and the great migration to Nevada it went into decline. Now the customers are coming back.'

Not in hordes, because Goodman cannot hope to compete with the corporate forces aligned against him, but there is a real sense of energy and optimism and significant changes have taken place. From being the seedy fight club it had become, a place where the best contests were often unscheduled affairs in the cheaper seats, the Garden is looking smart again and they are even wearing ties at ringside. The telephone rings more frequently in Goodman's office and he can pick from a better class of fighter.

'I think we are beginning to get somewhere,' he said, as winter continued to make its presence felt, the snow coming in sharp flurries to form on the streets of Manhattan. 'We are getting a lot of support, some encouraging corporate commitment and now it is a process of indoctrination.'

Translated from the American, which is not really English but a language manufactured on Wall Street and Madison Avenue, this means Goodman is attempting to persuade New Yorkers that there is more to boxing than a place on the dial. 'They lost the habit of coming here,' he said. This did not come about simply because big boxing had moved elsewhere; other reasons included bad fights, fighters who could not really fight and patrons who did not need much encouragement to show they were better equipped than the contestants. 'We have put this right,' added Goodman, who can now call upon not only better fighters but a less belligerent clientele. 'Plenty has happened here and I am beginning to hear again from managers who seemed to have forgotten our telephone number. We've got a good staff, a growing reputation and I think we can start to believe that there is a future for the Garden.'

Goodman is inspired by a sense of tradition, particularly when this relates to Mike Tyson, the heavyweight champion. If Tyson defended at the Garden, it would make him a part of the history in the way Ali, Frazier, Robinson and Dempsey are. They are synonymous with the Garden.

For a while, there was little profit in attempting to acquire such status. History was fine, but the New York taxes were crippling and mortgage companies do not accept Press clippings. New York no longer seemed to care about boxing, which is why boxing lost interest in New York.

Almost all boxing had left in the Garden was a ring, which turns out to be *the* ring. It is the very one in which Dempsey fought; in which Ali and Frazier staged a compelling struggle for the heavyweight championship; in which Ken Buchanan of Scotland proved that he was perhaps the most accomplished boxer to represent Britain since the Second World War.

The posts in the corners of that ring are made of brass, but their natural brightness is concealed beneath binding that protects television lenses from reflected glare. For Bobby Goodman they represent another time, symbols of what the Garden once was and if they are ever seen again in their full old-fashioned glory, he will know that the place is really back in business. ■

ROCKY MARCIANO

There were three reasons why Gerry Cooney (later to be a conspicuously inactive contender) was paid $5 million to challenge Larry Holmes for the heavyweight title on 11 June 1982, in Las Vegas. To begin with, Cooney was an impressively large and undeniably powerful young man. He could also punch. Then there was his complexion.

Cooney, a 25-year-old Irish-American from Huntington, Long Island, was unavoidably cast as the new white hope – a role originally associated with attempts to overthrow Jack Johnson, who encountered bitter racial prejudice after defeating Tommy Burns in 1910 to become the first black heavyweight champion.

As a result of the antagonism Johnson aroused, no black man was permitted to contest the title for 20 years after he lost it to Jess Willard in 1915. Although Joe Louis later developed into a national hero, Caucasian challengers could still count on widespread support by the time Joyce Carol Oates, a distinguished American novelist, wrote *On Boxing*, a serious study of the sport published in 1987.

> As recently as 1982, after decades of exemplary black boxers – from Jack Johnson to Joe Louis to Sugar Ray Robinson to Muhammad Ali – heavyweight champion Larry Holmes drew racist slurs and insults when he defended his title against the over-rated and overpromoted White Hope challenger Gerry Cooney (whose prefight picture, and not Holmes, ran on the cover of *Time* magazine). It is said that on the day of the match President Reagan's Secret Service installed a special telephone hookup in Cooney's dressing room so that the white boxer could be immediately congratulated if he won; there was no matching telephone in the black champion's dressing room.

This was never confirmed, but the merest sniff of Establishment bias was

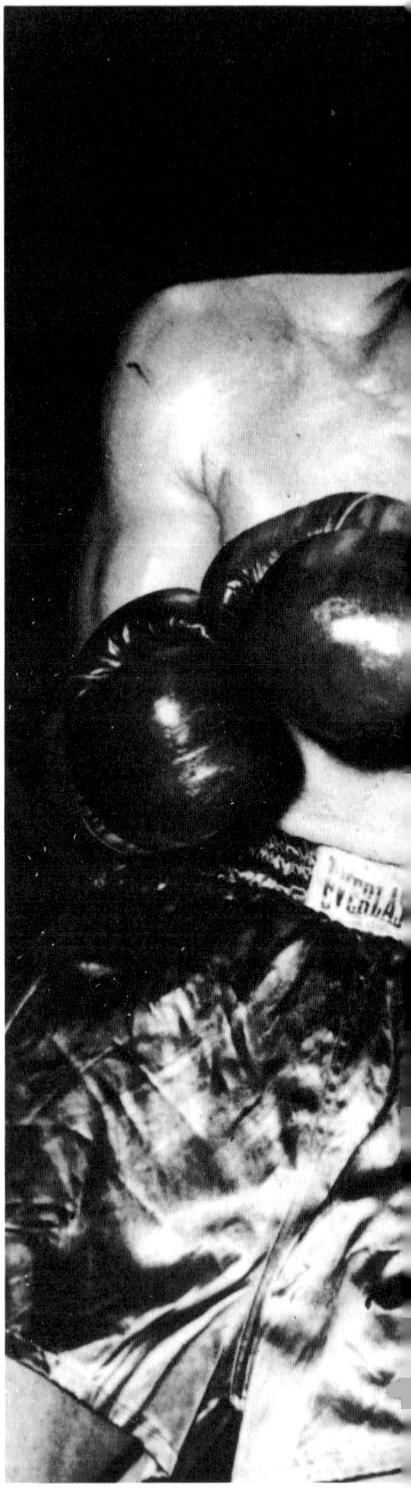

Rocky Marciano, the only heavyweight to retire undefeated. Born in Brockton, Massachusetts, he gained a reputation as the roughest of modern fighters, employing savage techniques that would probably have led to disqualification in European rings. Nobody who fought Marciano was ever the same again. Here, he powers in at Joe Louis who no longer had enough left to withstand the onslaught of a younger, stronger, man.

enough to rile Holmes who, when trying to equal Rocky Marciano's record, foolishly lashed out at the memory of the only heavyweight champion to retire undefeated.

Whatever else Marciano represented in Holmes's mind, his remarkable career exemplified white aspirations, an impression of indestructibility surviving the air crash that took his life in 1969. The late Red Smith wrote of him:

> The records make Rocky the best. In forty nine fights, nobody ever held him to a draw and only six opponents finished on their feet. Only one other heavyweight champion could show comparable figures: Gene Tunney, the most grievously underrated fighter of them all, lost once in seventy six bouts. Rocky Marciano couldn't box like Tunney and probably couldn't hit like Joe Louis, but in one respect he had no challenger. He was the toughest, strongest, most completely dedicated fighter who ever wore gloves. Fear wasn't in his vocabulary and pain had no meaning.

The grandson of an Italian blacksmith who emigrated to the United States from a village near Naples in 1914, Marciano was born Rocco Francesco Marchegiano, the eldest of six children, in Brockton, Massachusetts, on 1 September 1923. Nineteen months later, he almost died from pneumonia.

Raised during the Depression, but never on the breadline and responsive to parental and religious influences, Marciano attended Brockton High School, stayed out of serious trouble and was thought to have a future in baseball. It soon became clear that he had inherited great natural strength, but boxing did not figure in the future heavyweight champion's boyhood ambitions. As Izzy Gold said to Rocky

Marciano's biographer, Everett M. Skehan:

> The Rock never thought about being a boxer in those days. He didn't go to the YMCA or any of those places where they had kids involved in amateur boxing. Rock spent all his time practicing baseball. He never knew it was in the cards for him to be a pro fighter. If Rocky had ever suspected he was going to be a fighter, he'd have been working at it from the time he was ten years old . . . There were guys around Brockton who were bigger and better built than Rock, but they didn't have his determination and guts. The Rock was always first to take a chance at something we were trying to prove we weren't afraid of. He'd jump a river, climb a tree, swim across a lake, fight a kid three years older than him. I always knew he'd be a winner. He was the kind of kid who wouldn't allow himself to lose. But I figured he'd be a winner in baseball.

Marciano did appear as a semi-professional in the minor leagues while working in factories and then with a construction crew, clearing sites for army barracks; but in 1943 he was drafted and served in Europe for two years as a combat engineer, ferrying supplies across the English Channel to Normandy.

Before Marciano was demobbed and when stationed at Fort Lewis, Washington, he began to box regularly for his unit and so began an extraordinary tale. There had to be something better than the shoe factories and the pervasive smell of leather never leaving his nostrils, better than the ditches and building sites and men shaking their heads when he asked about a job. There was money in boxing and the heavyweight championship was the richest prize in sport.

Marciano did not look the part; his body had grown soft. He had heavy legs and short arms; he was only 5 ft 10 in and a fondness for pasta

BENLEE

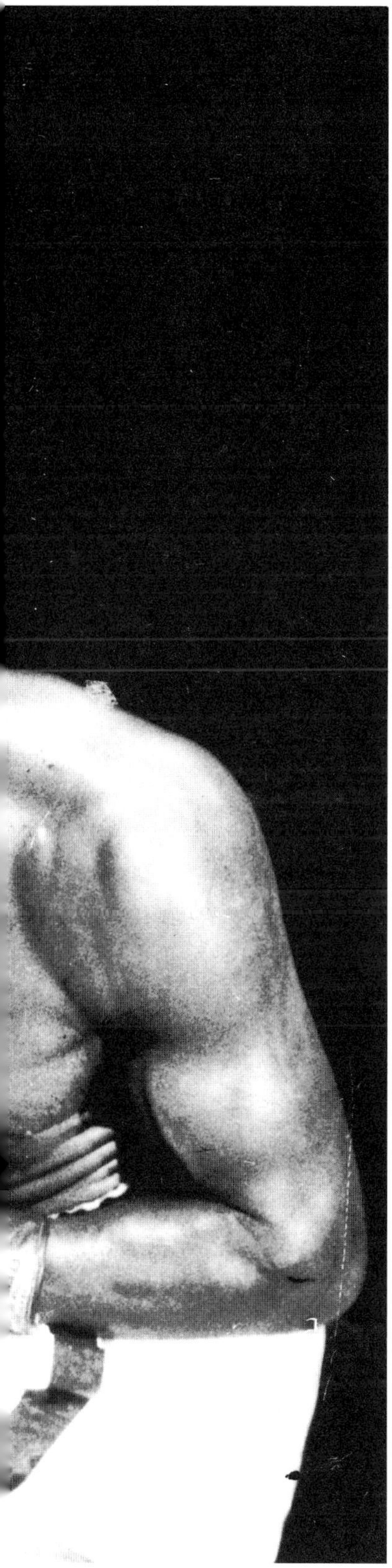

Marciano became Champion in September 1952 with a 13-round knock-out of Jersey Joe Walcott in Philadelphia. Walcott fought with great skill and courage and more than held his own until the challenger caught him with a terrible right in the thirteenth round.

and wine had filled out his gut. He fought crudely, with no respect for the rules, and was booed out of the ring after being disqualified against Henry Lester, a former Golden Gloves champion who was sent down by a knee to the groin. People in boxing looked at Marciano, then 23, and shook their heads.

Joe Cirelli, a professional trainer, said: 'Forget it. You're too old to be starting out. You're not tall enough. Your arms are too short and your legs are too thick. Forget boxing. You'd get killed in the pros.'

In May 1947 Marciano turned back to baseball, but failed to impress the Chicago Cubs after spending three weeks at their training camp in North Carolina.

It is not unusual for people to fantasize about their athletic past, believing in middle age that they were thwarted only by lack of opportunity; but a fundamental difference between casual and serious sport is perhaps best explained by Roger Khan in *The Boys of Summer*. As a young reporter in the early Fifties, he was assigned to cover the Brooklyn Dodgers and recalls standing over the plate, adopting a batting stance to help pitcher Carl Labine with his control.

> Walker [the catcher] squatted and Labine threw a sinker. Although Labine was not regarded as very fast, and was complaining about his arm, the ball exploded past the plate with a sibilant whoosh, edged by a buzzing as of hornets. I had never heard a thrown ball make that sound before. The ball seemed to accelerate as it came closer; an accelerating, impossibly fast pitch that made the noises of hornets and snakes.

Khan was warned not to move, to stand perfectly still.

> Labine threw a dozen sinkers, closer to me, and after that began to break his

curve. Because of certain aerodynamic principles, a righthanded pitcher's curve starts toward a righthanded batter's left ear. I watched the baseball approach. It closed with me. I was paralyzed. Then, at what seemed the last millisecond, the spinning ball grabbed air and hooked away from my head and over the plate – the impulse was not simply to duck but to throw away the bat and throw my body to the thick-bladed Florida grass. I could no more have swung, let alone hit, one of Labine's pitches than run a three-minute mile. All the baseball I had played was irrelevant to sinkers that hissed like snakes and curves that paralyzed.

Marciano was better equipped than Khan to cope with the reality of professional baseball, but not good enough to be considered a prospect in the major leagues; boxing beckoned again and despite losing four of 12 amateur contests, a friend, Allie Columbo, recommended him to Al Weill.

Weill, a man of Pickwickian proportions and much cunning, made matches for the International Boxing Club at Madison Square Garden and was known to be an associate of Frankie Carbo and Blinky Palermo, gangsters who wielded considerable influence in American boxing until exposed by the Kefauver Commission on Organized Crime. He had managed fighters for most of his adult life, including three world champions and Arturo Godoy, a limited but naturally quarrelsome Chilean who gave Joe Louis two hard fights when challenging for the heavyweight championship.

Before Weill agreed to handle Marciano, he sent him to Charley Goldman, a tiny 60-year-old English-born trainer whose gnarled features and misshapen hands were the result of more than 300 contests as a professional bantamweight. Goldman needed none of his vast experience to identify Marciano as a crude brawler; but Marciano could punch and there was encouraging evidence of an immense will. 'We might be able to do something with him,' Goldman said to Weill.

Marciano signed with Weill and from Goldman he learned how to exploit strength, power and determination. Opponents knew they could outbox Marciano and he was frequently embarrassed by their manoeuvres; but it was only a matter of time before they were worn down and all but six were either knocked out or battered into submission.

No fighter in history has been more astutely managed and Marciano's willingness to endure extremes of spartan preparation is embedded in the folklore of the game. Carefully matched by Weill, he recorded 24 straight victories – 22 inside the distance, 19 before the third round was completed.

In common with a number of outstanding champions, Marciano had a gentle nature, but once inside the ring he responded completely to a primal instinct, frequently employing rough-house tactics that would have led to instant disqualification in Europe.

It is said that Marciano took more out of his opponents than any fighter in history and there is plenty of evidence to suggest none of them were ever the same after going in with him. This was certainly true of Carmine Vingo, an Italian-American from the Bronx, who gave Marciano his first serious test on 30 December 1949 at Madison Square Garden. Down in each of the first two rounds, Vingo recovered to shake Marciano but was struck senseless in the sixth and, to the victor's horror, did not regain consciousness for a week.

After defeating Roland La Starza on a close and controversial split decision at the Garden on 24 March 1950, Marciano fought seven times in New England before returning to New York for what was thought to

Marciano lashed out at anything he saw in the ring, often taking severe punishment in order to achieve an advantage. He never seemed to have an easy fight. With blood seeping from a cut over his left eye, he rattles Ezzard Charles's jaw with a powerful right.

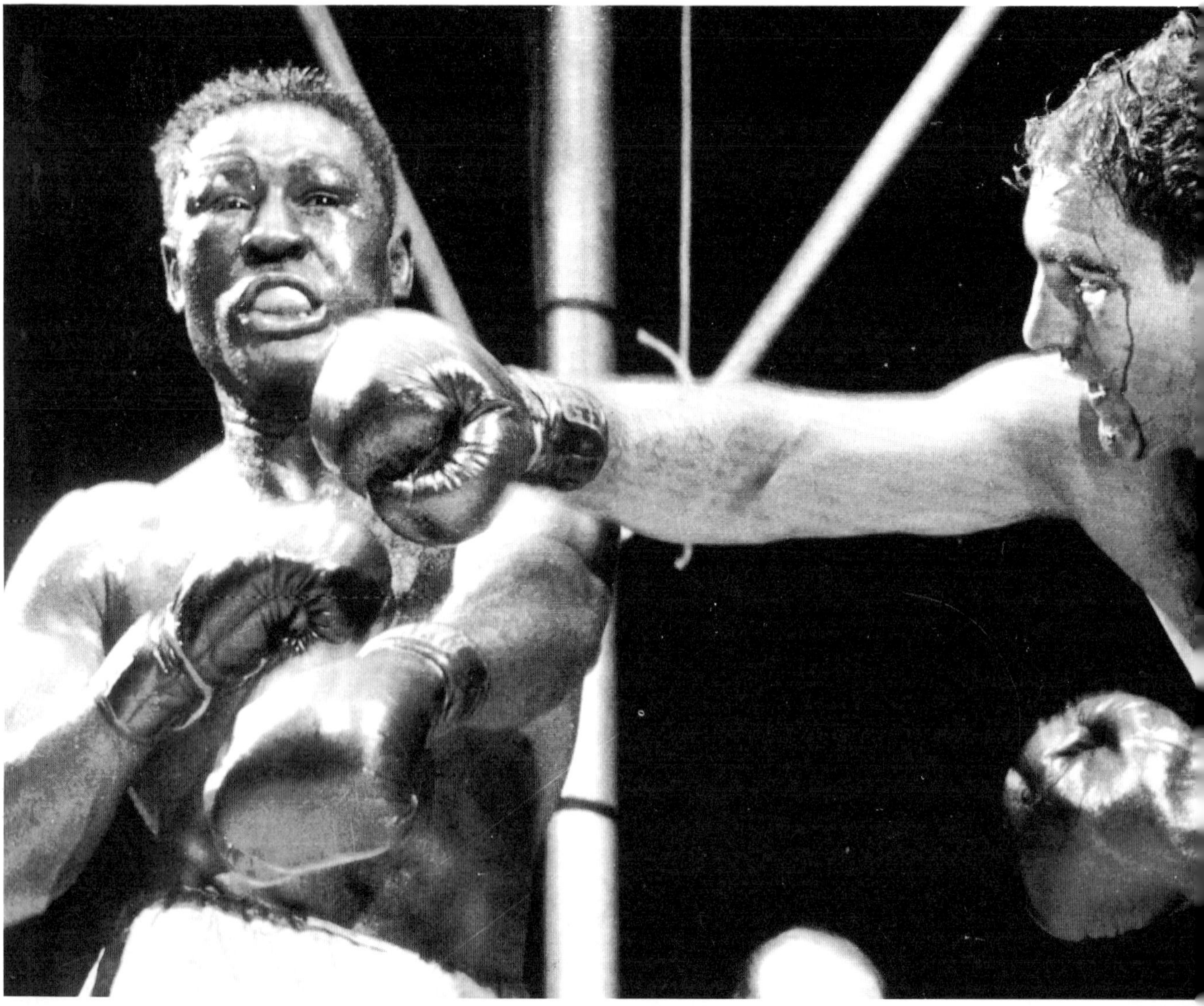

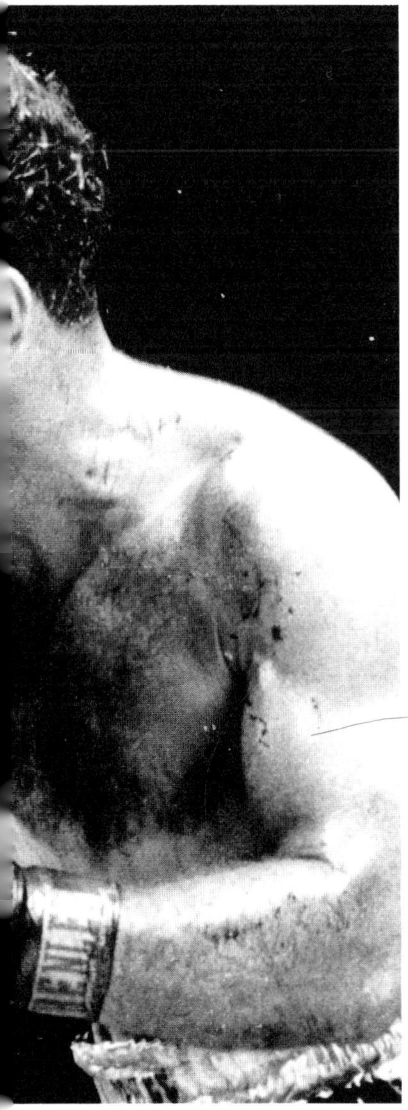

be a difficult contest against Rex Layne. It lasted just six rounds. Freddie Beshore, a former National Boxing Association contender, lasted two rounds fewer. Then, on 26 October 1951, Marciano was matched with Joe Louis.

Louis, perhaps the greatest of all heavyweight champions had been forced back into the ring by financal imperatives. He was 37, balding and flabby but still immensely popular, suffering none of the racial discrimination then still manifest in American sport; black players, most notably Jackie Robinson, had begun to appear in the major baseball leagues, but as the *Sporting News* concluded in 1952 (a year after Marciano and Louis fought): 'It is reasonably certain that there are some clubs which prefer to operate with all-white casts.'

It was irrefutably true that many Americans relished the prospects of a white heavyweight champion, the first since James J. Braddock in 1937, but there was widespread respect and sympathy for Louis who had carefully avoided controversy, preferring to represent his race as a great and dignified sportsman.

As with Mike Tyson, in a later era, most of Louis's opponents were intimidated before they went to the ring and yet, interestingly, he was always easy to hit and went down many times. Max Schmeling, Jersey Joe Walcott, Buddy Baer and Two-Ton Tony Galento had all embarrassed Louis in that fashion, but keeping him down was a different proposition. Gifted with sharp reflexes and great power, Louis could do terrible damage at close range and until the years settled on him, he never conceded initiative. Now he was old.

The future made grim by accumulating interest on back taxes, Louis came out of retirement in 1950 and lost a 15-round decision to Ezzard Charles for the vacant championship. He had won eight in a row since then, but time waits for no fighter and a harsh drama was about to unfold.

'Pain had no meaning for him.' Rocky Marciano stages a ferocious rally to stop Roland La Starza in the 11th round on 24 September 1953.

Although Louis went to his corner much the taller and heavier man, vastly more experienced and with a nine-inch reach advantage, he knew that Marciano would force the pace, oblivious to pain, absorbing stiff punches in order to deliver his own.

For the first time in his career, Louis had to retreat and at the end of the seventh, referee Ruby Goldstein had Marciano ahead – four rounds to two and one even; both the judges, Joe Angelo and Harold Barnes, also favoured Marciano.

A left hook put Louis down in the next round and though he was up at eight, there were clear signs of dishevelment as Marciano renewed his relentless assault. Eyes vacant, legs quivering, Louis was driven to the ropes, where he took two more savage hooks. Then a chilling right ripped into his jaw. He fell backwards through the ropes and after counting to four, Goldstein signalled that the fight was over.

Marciano had mixed emotions. The thrill of victory was set against admiration for a noble figure, and before leaving the dressing-room he sent Louis a respectful note.

Archie Moore, bottom left, by then almost 40 years old, knocked Marciano down in the first round when they met in the Heavyweight Championship in New York on 21 September 1955 and claimed that the Champion benefited from a long count. Marciano recovered to knock out Moore in the ninth round.

People who rise to prominence from disadvantaged birth often become obsessed with wealth and Marciano's eagerness to accumulate hard cash, seen eventually as inveterate meanness, remains legendary. It is said that some of his money, buried in tin cans, has never been recovered, the secret gone to the grave.

On the other hand, there can be no doubt that Marciano was wickedly exploited by Weill, who not only took 50 per cent of his purses but conspired against him with Jim Norris, President of the International Boxing Commission and the most influential figure in Ameri-

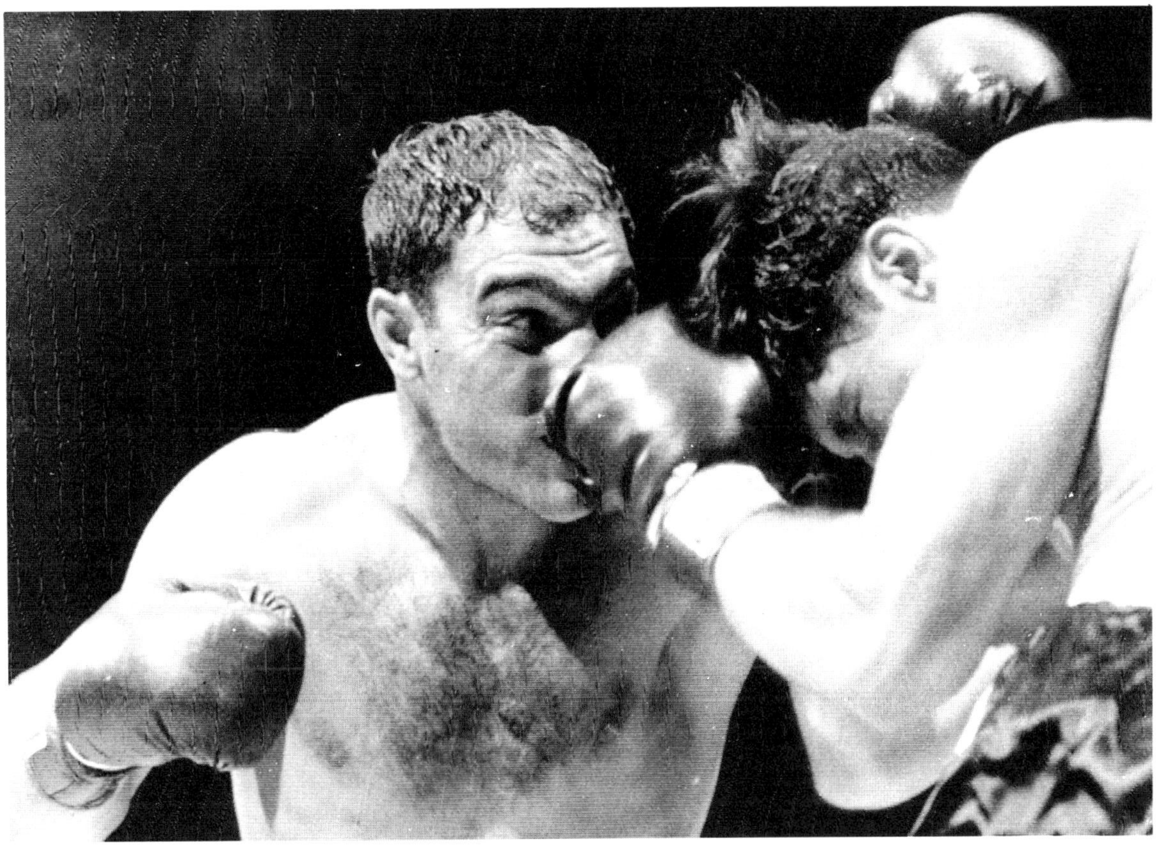

can boxing. Instead of promoting Marciano's interests, Weill readily agreed to step aside so that Jersey Joe Walcott could defend the heavyweight title against Ezzard Charles. Walcott had signed exclusively with the IBC, an ironic arrangement in view of the frustration he had experienced when thought to be the next best heavyweight to Louis.

Walcott outpointed Charles on 5 June 1952 and Marciano could no longer be kept out of the picture. They came together on 23 September in Philadelphia. There could be no conceivable doubt about Walcott's credentials. Officially 38 years old, he was probably more than 40 but possessed sound technique and substantial reserves of energy.

Before the opening round could be completed, Marciano was down for the first time in his career. He had expected Walcott to retreat from a predictable onslaught. Instead the champion came forward, throwing punches with both hands. After little more than a minute of frenzied activity, Walcott landed a left hook and the challenger went over on to his left side. Up at three, blazing with indignation, he launched savage counter-attacks and by the end of the sixth both men were bleeding.

Each time Marciano returned to the corner, his handlers expressed their accumulating anxiety, becoming so excitable that, when attempting to staunch gaping wounds, they almost blinded him with a carelessly applied astringent. The contest was proving far more difficult than had been imagined and they were no longer confident about the outcome. Far from wilting, Walcott appeared to be growing stronger and easily avoided Marciano's uninspired rushes.

By the end of the twelfth, the challenger was a mess: blood seeping from cuts around his eyes, his lips and a gash in his scalp. Walcott was undoubtedly ahead and there was only one way Marciano could win.

'How am I doing?' he asked.

'You're losing,' he was told. 'You'll have to knock him out.'

During more than 20 years of prize-fighting, Walcott had discovered that by swaying back on the ropes he could then use the released torque to energize a surprise counter-attack. Gaining in confidence and probably trying to further emphasize his superiority by repeating the hook that dropped Marciano in the opening round, Walcott retreated and, when feeling his shoulder-blades against the strands, attempted to spring the trap. Before he could catapult forward, Marciano delivered a short right with such pulverizing force that the champion's face became a grotesque mask of distorted tissue; Skehan wrote:

> As Walcott crumpled, Marciano came around with a looping left that grazed his head. But the punch was not needed. The champion sank to one knee, his left arm hooked around the middle rope, his head resting on the canvas. Marciano ran for his corner. But the fight was over. The referee could have counted to ten hundred, Walcott never moved. And finally, when it no longer mattered, he had to be helped to his corner.

More than a quarter of a century later, Walcott, still sprightly and a frequent visitor to the ringside in Atlantic City, recalled the extent of his disappointment:

> Rocky had youth and energy on his side and was so strong that I knew my only real chance was to win a decision. But I can't think of another important fight when I felt more confident. Putting Rocky down in the first round was a big thing and by the time we got to half way there wasn't a doubt left in my mind. Then he hit me with that right . . . a tremendous

punch. It's understandable why people think of Rocky as a great champion. He was extraordinary because he didn't understand pain.

Huge crowds turned out when Marciano returned to Brockton and news of his victory caused great excitement in Italy.

Within three months, Marciano was back in training for a return with Walcott, scheduled for Chicago on 10 April 1953, but then postponed until 15 May because of an injury to his nose. This time Walcott lasted just 2 minutes 25 seconds, claiming in the ring that he had beaten the count after being lifted off his feet by a right uppercut. It was not the most plausible of explanations for such an abrupt end to the proceedings and some experienced observers of boxing were inclined to suspect that Marciano had effectively ended Walcott's career six months earlier, so undermining the former champion's morale that he no longer possessed the will to withstand heavy punches to the head. Walcott never fought again.

The contest did little to embellish Marciano's reputation and nothing for his relationship with Weill, who blamed Jim Norris for an astonishing discrepancy in purse money. As champion, Marciano was paid $166,030, almost $100,000 less than Walcott. That apart, those closest to Marciano began to sense he was becoming disenchanted with fierce self-imposed disciplines without which he could not hope to sustain a raw fighting style.

The first of five subsequent defences took place at the Polo Grounds, New York, on 24 September 1953: a re-match with Roland La Starza, who had taken him to a close decision three years earlier. Outclassed for six rounds, falling further and further behind, more frustrated than ever before in his professional career, Marciano showed such utter contempt for the rules that he lost the sixth round on a foul and ought to have been disqualified.

Confronted with another crisis, Marciano once again reached into his great reservoir of strength and will. The majority of fighters favour specific targets: the chin, the heart, the lower ribs, the abdomen; Marciano simply struck out at whatever he could see or thought he could reach – his belief in brute force so absolute, so savagely applied that many of his opponents were inclined to feel they should have been issued with a breastplate and a helmet.

Those who attempted to cover up behind their gloves risked paralysing shock from blows that wearied and eventually brought down their arms – as La Starza discovered again when Marciano renewed the offensive, fighting with such primitive ferocity that even veteran ringsiders gasped in amazement. From being clearly ahead, La Starza quickly fell behind, reeling before the champion's brutalizing attacks, the outcome now inevitable. It was stopped in the eleventh.

Many people in boxing think of Ezzard Charles as an outstanding heavyweight who deserves to be better remembered. Born in Lawrenceville, Georgia, on 7 July 1921, he won 96 of 122 professional contests and was only 54 when he died on 27 May 1975 in Chicago.

Stylish and technically correct, he outpointed Walcott to win the vacant National Boxing Association heavyweight championship in June 1949 and held it for almost two years. Three decades later Larry Holmes, an excellent and considerably underrated champion, found it difficult to escape from the shadow of Muhammad Ali. Charles had a similar experience. He defeated a much diminished Joe Louis for the undisputed title in 1950 but was unfortunate to be of the same era.

Charles lost the championship when Walcott knocked him out in the seventh round on 18 July 1952 and was then outpointed in a return. By the following year he appeared to be an ideal opponent for Marciano. There had been a hint of weariness about his work and at 33 he was three years older than the champion. When they came together at the Yankee Stadium in New York on 17 June 1954, with Marciano an odds-on favourite, Charles was given little chance of surviving the full 15 rounds. He was still there at the final bell.

Described as one of the best-ever heavyweight contests, it not only emphasized that Charles had every right to think of himself as an outstanding figure in the division, but it also raised further questions about Marciano's future. For all his immense strength, he could no longer be relied on to overwhelm craftier opponents quickly and the rift with Weill was widening.

After holding his own for three rounds, Charles then opened a terrible cut at the side of Marciano's left eye that would have completely demoralized a lesser man. Two inches long and an inch deep, it continued to gush blood, worsening with each round, despite frantic administrations in the corner.

During the minute that separates rounds, the corner-men apply themselves to specific tasks. The manager or trainer advises and cajoles. His assistant attends to the fighter's body, wiping him down, removing and rinsing the gum-shield, perhaps smearing grease on facial abrasions. The cut man stands by in case of a crisis.

In an outstanding anthology, first published in 1982, Hugh McIlvanney of the *Observer* wrote:

> Corner-men in this country [Britain] find cuts particularly menacing because they are not allowed to treat their boxers with anything more

Don Cockell, barely more than a light-heavyweight, took a terrible beating when he challenged Marciano in San Francisco on 16 May 1955.

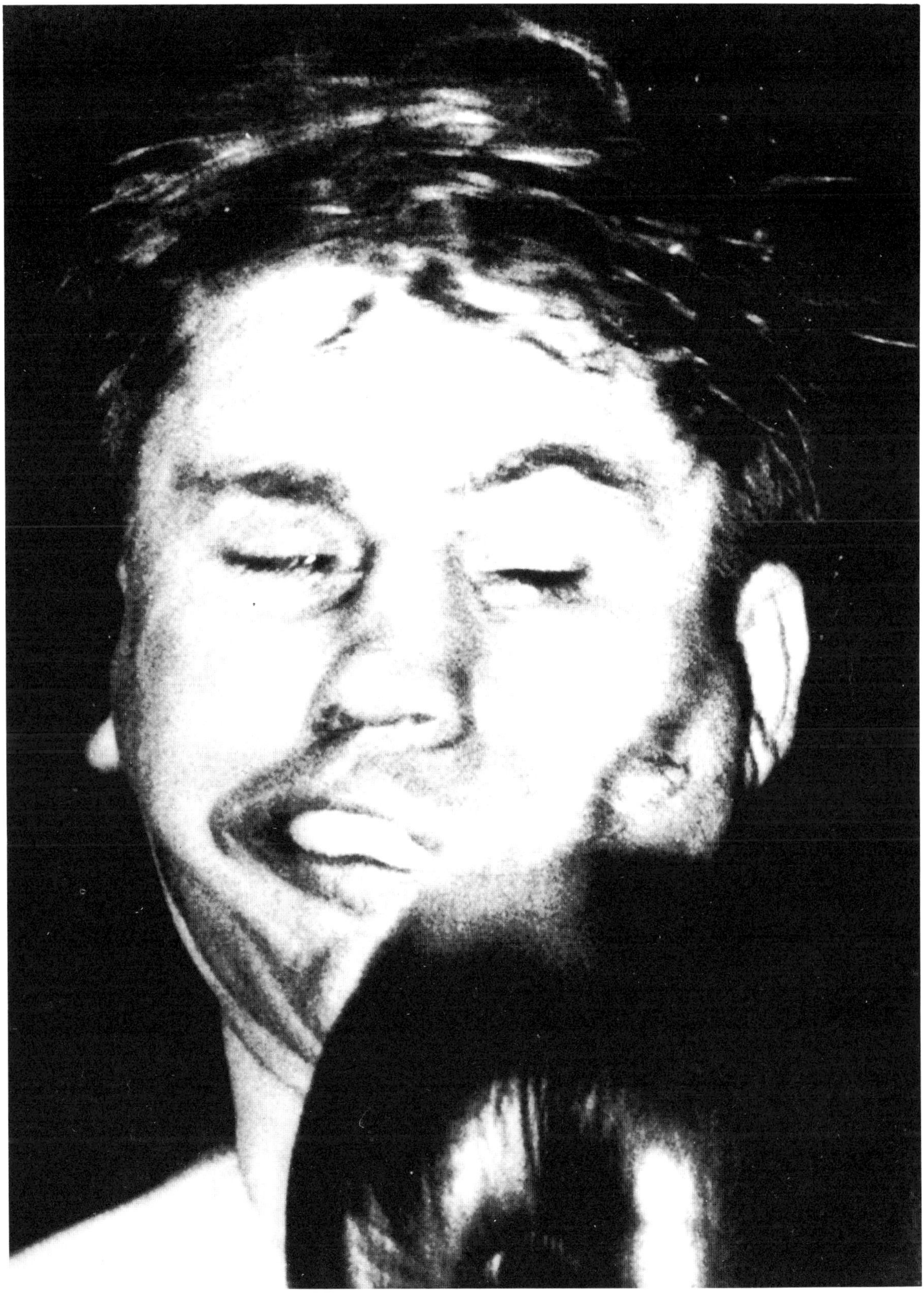

> powerful than an adrenalin solution of one in a thousand. In America where there is less official concern about the long-term effects of ringside operations, seconds employ substances that would damn a river. Willie Ketchum, an old-time manager, uses a cement-like preparation that has to be laboriously chipped out of the wound after a fight. 'The fighter gets cut, I stop it,' Ketchum says flatly. 'After I've worked on it you could shoot the sonofabitch and he wouldn't bleed.' Needless to say, the ultimate results of such methods are less than decorative.

Marciano's rough-house tactics are obvious from this sequence of pictures. Don Cockell attempts to shove off the champion but is unable to prevent him boring in and is clearly hurt by a head butt.

Marciano's cut man was Freddie Brown, whose expertise was still thought to be invaluable more than 25 years later when he was persuaded out of retirement to work with Roberto Duran. Brown cannot recall dealing with a wound worse than the one he had to treat in Marciano's corner and had the contest not been for the heavyweight championship, it would surely have been stopped.

Even by his own exceptional standards of courage and determination, the effect on Marciano was remarkable. Making no attempt to protect the eye, he carried the fight to Charles, his face a crimson mask, scowling through the hurt as stinging jabs and sharp counters leaped in to his face. Now Charles began to weaken and by the end of the ninth round he was fortunate to be still upright.

When they came up for the final session, Marciano was ahead, but he fought as though the decision remained in doubt, trying desperately to achieve a knock-out. The scoring was unanimously in his favour.

Marciano's biographer quotes the referee, Ruby Goldstein:

> Charles was a very good, smart fighter, who still employed the tactics he had as a middleweight. He gave Marciano trouble for the first ten rounds. He came at him fast with an assortment of punches, and he hit Rocky with

a lot of combinations where he'd put together five or six punches in a row. Most fighters would grab on and wait for their head to clear after being hit by a good combination. But this is where Marciano was a discouraging-type fighter. After a fighter hit him with some of his best punches, Rocky would come chasing right after him, back him up against the ropes, and throw seven or eight punches of his own.

The return on 17 September further emphasized how much Marciano took out of his opponents. Charles simply was not the same man who had stood up so valiantly three months earlier, but he still managed to inflict a terrible injury – the worst of Marciano's career.

Realizing he was way behind, Charles rallied in the sixth round and split Marciano's left nostril, the wound so horribly severe that his handlers feared the contest would be stopped. They pleaded with the Commission doctor and Marciano was allowed to continue, blood spurting again when a punch dislodged a swab, deliberately left, in his nose.

Charles tried to concentrate his attacks on the torn flesh, but he was in the presence of a temporary primitive who refused to yield. Amazingly Marciano took the seventh, but the word was that he would be allowed only one more.

With 24 seconds of the eighth round remaining, Charles was counted out. He had survived one knock-down but he could not withstand the next bludgeoning assault.

It was a while before Marciano recovered, the wound slow to heal and there was time to look around for the next challenger. The choice fell on Don Cockell, the British heavyweight champion.

Cockell, a 26-year-old former blacksmith from Surrey, did not look the part, but his Bunterish shape was the result of a glandular disorder rather than negligence. He had beaten Harry 'Kid' Matthews and La Starza and was five years younger than the champion. Nevertheless, Marciano could not get excited about the prospect, believing Cockell to be the least-threatening contender he had been offered.

Weill and Goldman grew nervous. They recognized a change in Marciano, not so much a diminishment of his remarkable powers as a lack of enthusiasm, and they expressed anger and concern when a sparring partner knocked him down. They knew that he had to be totally a fighter, otherwise he might be in trouble, even against mediocre opposition.

For a couple of rounds at the Kezar Stadium in San Francisco on 16 May 1955, Cockell did well, but from then on took a terrible beating. Aware that Marciano was instinctively the dirtiest great fighter of his time, Cockell had promised to meet foul with foul. 'If he butts me then I'll butt him back. If he hits me low I'll hit him lower. If he lands after the bell I'll do the same.'

It proved to be an empty threat. Brawling came naturally to the champion and he violated every known rule, once hitting Cockell when he was down. Towards the end of the eighth round, a stunning right sent Cockell through the ropes and on to the ring apron. By the ninth he was utterly exhausted, bruised and cut. He had nothing left but his fighting heart; as Marciano advanced again, referee Frankie Brown jumped between them and took Cockell in his arms.

Marciano was now convinced that he was being cheated by Weill, but they stayed together for what was to be the last defence.

Born in Benoit, Mississippi, on 13 December 1913, Archie Moore became unquestionably one of the most astonishing figures in boxing history, his career developing into a defiant stand against the inexorable passage of time. In 1962, when but a few weeks short of his forty-ninth birthday, Moore lost to the young Cassius Clay. He held the light-heavyweight championship for many years and married four times. He took part in 229 official contests and set a record of 126 knock-outs. Nobody has brought more cunning to the ring. On 21 September 1955, then 42, he went nine rounds with Marciano.

Moore had been pressing his claim for almost a year and more than 60,000 showed up at the Yankee Stadium in New York. They were not disappointed.

It was thought inconceivable that Moore would be able to withstand Marciano's relentless surges for 15 rounds or that his exaggerated ego would permit a negative strategy, so many people believed he would try to knock out the champion, an unlikely but nevertheless intriguing possibility.

How Moore might achieve this miracle was still being debated when he delivered a solid right that sent Marciano down on one knee. It was only the second time the champion had experienced such embarrassment and he was immediately in peril of being taken apart by one of the deadliest finishers boxing has ever known. Dazed, he rose instinctively at two, but the referee, Harry Kessler, forgetting a rule change, continued with the count, thereby denying Moore an opportunity to prosper from the advantage.

The chance had gone. Moore continued to pick off Marciano, but there was an inevitability about the outcome which was confirmed when the challenger went down twice in the sixth round. At the end of the eighth, a fierce session during which both men came under heavy fire, Marciano sent Moore down again. Saved by the bell, he was given an opportunity to surrender. 'I'll go down fighting,' he said.

The end came early in the ninth. Moore came out and fought with all his remaining strength, but he was battered by a wild volley of punches and counted out. It was the last time Marciano would know such elation.

Almost exactly seven months later, on 27 April 1956, Marciano announced his retirement, the only heavyweight to do so undefeated. Forty-nine fights, 49 victories: the perfect record. 'There were a number of reasons why he quit,' said one of Marciano's brothers, Sonny. 'But the absolute main one was Al Weill. He just hated the guy and didn't trust him.'

At 6 p.m. on Sunday 31 August 1969, Glenn Blez, a comparatively inexperienced pilot, took off in a Cessna from Chicago Airport and headed for Des Moines, Iowa. He had two passengers, both friends. The one alongside him had been heavyweight champion of the world. A little more than three hours later, all three were dead. Rescuers found Marciano's battered body still strapped in the seat of the wrecked aircraft.

When people in boxing heard about this, they remembered what a writer said when Staney Ketchel, the great middleweight champion, was shot and killed: 'Start counting ten over him. He'll get up.' ■

SUGAR RAY ROBINSON

Fighters are not inclined to dwell on the immediacy of pain, the sudden clamour of departing consciousness that results from a savage blow to the head, the chilling realization that some good men did not make it back from oblivion.

In June 1947, in his first defence of the world welterweight championship, Sugar Ray Robinson knocked out Jimmy Doyle in the eighth round; Doyle, from Cleveland, died in hospital.

'Did you intend to hurt the deceased?' Robinson was asked at the inquest.

'That, sir, is what I'm paid to do,' he replied.

People who believed professional boxing to be uncivilized and exploitive were offended by Robinson's matter-of-fact response; but far from being callous or attempting to avoid all responsibility for the first death to occur in a championship bout for more than 50 years, he was merely stating an unavoidable truth about the one sport that ought never to be spoken of as a game.

When you come to look at the life and career of Ray Robinson, there is no way of denying that if he is not the best boxer who ever lived, then he is as near to it as we are ever likely to know. Between 1940 and 1965 he had 201 professional contests and 12 of only 19 defeats came after he had turned 40. Unbeaten as welterweight champion, he won the middleweight title five times and, but for heat exhaustion, would have taken the light-heavyweight championship from Joey Maxim at the Yankee Stadium, New York, in June 1952.

A video collection of Robinson's greatest fights reveals startling technique, tremendous will and impressive dignity. In victory he simply raised one hand; disappointments were accepted with a gracious nod. He was never knocked out and 109 opponents failed to go the distance.

Despite his superior technique, Sugar Ray Robinson failed to take the Light-heavyweight Championship from Joey Maxim on 25 June 1952. When the fighters went to the ring the temperature at the Yankee Stadium New York was more than 100°F and referee Ruby Goldstein suffered so much that he was replaced by a substitute official. Robinson was clearly ahead on points when he retired with heat exhaustion: the twelfth round.

Eddie Futch speaks about Robinson with admiration and absolute respect. A veteran American trainer who has worked with 16 world champions, including Joe Frazier, Ken Norton, Michael Spinks and Marlon Starling, he said: 'It is not unusual nowadays for a kid to get a title shot before he has learned enough about the business. By the time Ray got that far, and of course it took longer in those days, he knew almost everything there is to know, he had marvellous balance, speed, superb reflexes and was just as dangerous with either hand when going backwards.'

Reg Gutteridge, the ITV boxing commentator, who covered many of Robinson's fights, remains in awe of him. 'I never ceased to be amazed, yes, thrilled by his technique,' he wrote in *The Big Punchers*. 'The way he could feint an opponent into a mistake and execute the counter punch; a right hand to disturb a southpaw-style rival; slipping inside a left lead and whipping a left hook; the short, sharp right or the more spectacular uppercut. His was the perfect example of punch delivery, being sufficient to down an opponent without needing the power possessed by so-called natural big hitters.'

Born Walker Smith Junior in a dilapidated tenement building in Detroit, Michigan, on 3 May 1920, the youngest of three children, Robinson was only 6 when his parents divorced. He shined shoes, delivered newspapers and fought other hungry boys for the best odd jobs. Thanks to his mother, Leila, whose father and grandfather were Georgia plantation slaves, Robinson and two elder sisters received an education and he first learned to box at the Brewster Community Centre.

Many of the stories told about Robinson's youth are apocryphal. They say that he busked in the streets around Broadway, tap-dancing for the theatre crowds, and that he was encouraged by Bojangles Bill Robinson who paid weekly visits to Harlem. They also say that he could do a perfect imitation of the great dancer.

By then, Leila Smith had moved her small family to New York. As a teenager Robinson began to fight regularly in Police Athletic League boxing tournaments and on the streets he was a handful. In an early biography, Gene Schoor quotes Warren Murphy describing sorties to a tough neighbourhood, Chelsea Park. 'Me and Smitty would hook rides down there and every time we knew we were in for it. The kids around Chelsea resented outsiders and they swarmed all over us. And did we fight! You had a chance if you knew how to use your fists. I used to be pretty good. But Junior – he was hell on wheels.'

At just 15 and weighing barely seven stone, Robinson already looked an exceptional talent, quick footed and an impressively sharp puncher. No one saw this more clearly than George Gainford, who became not only Robinson's mentor but surrogate father. Gainford took him to amateur and professional shows, pointing out the strengths and weaknesses of various fighters and the problems imposed by different styles.

One night in Waterbury, Connecticut, a junior featherweright failed to show up. Robinson wanted to fight but did not possess the mandatory AAU card, so he borrowed one from a young boxer, Ray Robinson. An instant success, he was no longer Walker Smith Junior and when it was suggested his style was sweet as sugar, that too became a part of legend. Now he was Sugar Ray Robinson.

Unbeaten as an amateur, Robinson won 125 contests and the official record shows 69 knock-outs, 44 of them in the first round. He won the Golden Gloves featherweight championship in 1939 and became lightweight champion the following year.

After being dragged to his corner, Robinson was placed on his stool, and had to be assisted to the dressing-room.

Twenty-five years later, Robinson – tall, handsome and flamboyant – would have been a sensation instantly, a natural television star, benefiting hugely from an expansion in the communications business. Denied that exposure and in order to advance his career, Robinson, with Gainford's support, agreed to box for Kurt Horrman, a wealthy brewer and amateur sportsman who had considerable influence in New York.

The relationship, always fragile, came to an end in 1942. Robinson bought out the contract for $10,000 and Gainford, who had been retained to train him, was reappointed manager.

Already established as a major force in the welterweight division, Robinson continued to make spectacular progress and in October 1942 began a long feud with Jake La Motta, a crude but effective fighter from the Bronx district of New York, whose autobiography, *Raging Bull*, was turned into a successful movie. Robinson, giving away almost a stone in weight, won a ten-round decision but lost the return on 5 February 1943. It was his first defeat. A month later Robinson became Private Walker Smith Junior, United States Army.

Robinson served for little more than a year and plenty of barbed questions were asked when he was discharged because of a punctured ear-drum. Suddenly he was no longer popular and appointed Pete Vacarre, a New York boxing writer, as Press agent. Together with Gainford, they set about clearing a path towards the welterweight championship. Titles had been frozen for the duration but Mike Jacobs, then the controlling force in American boxing, promised Robinson a chance once Freddie Cochrane, the 10 st 7 lb champion, came out of the navy.

Robinson had effectively been the champion since 1941 but was

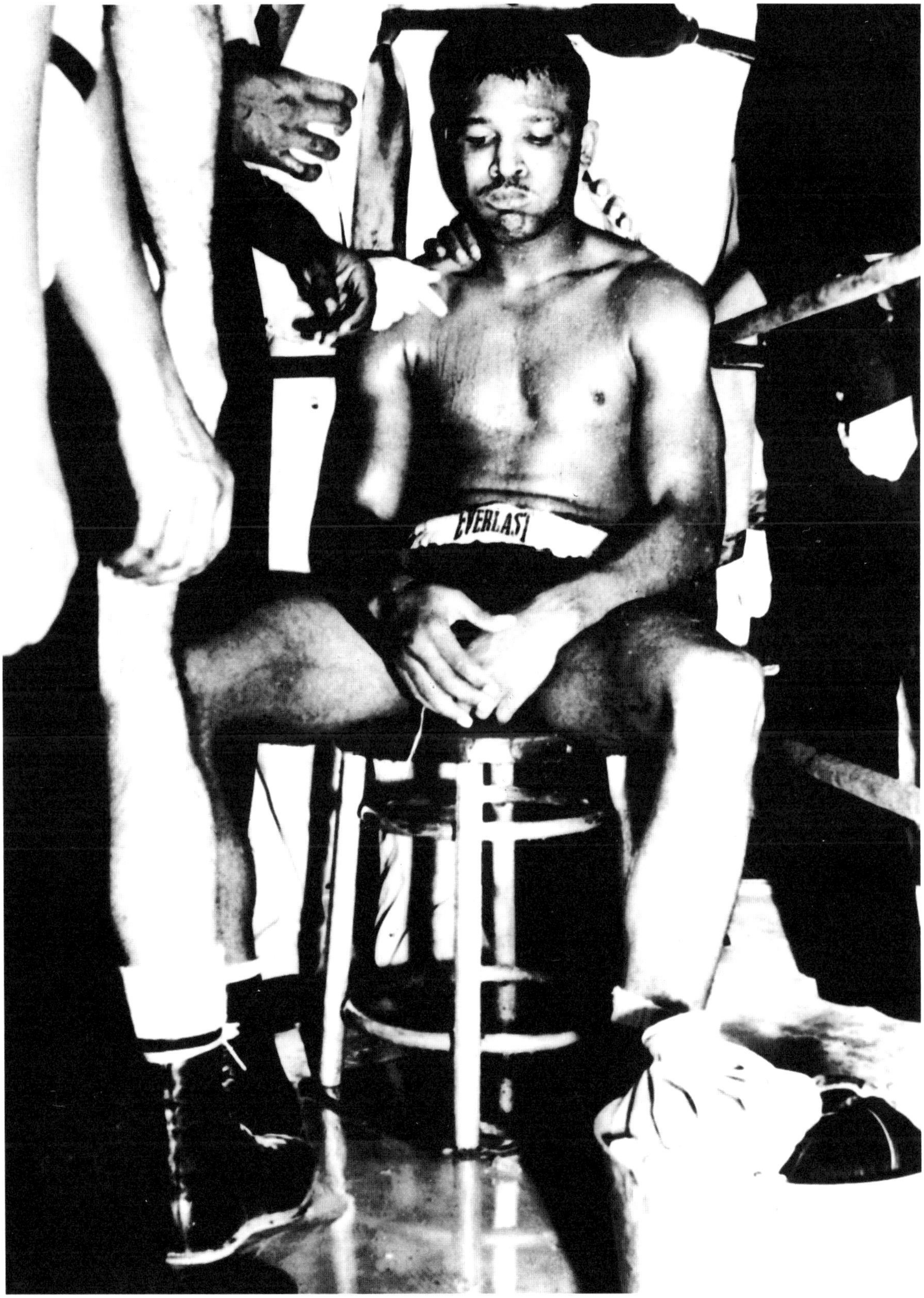
EVERLAST

side-tracked when Cochrane chose to defend against Marty Servo, who knocked him out in the fourth round. Four days before he was due to meet Robinson, Servo called off with an injured nose. The New York State commission declared the title vacant and then, astonishingly, ordered an elimination tournament. Robinson at last became champion on 20 December 1946, outpointing Tommy Bell at Madison Square Garden, New York, and boxing for the fifteenth time that year.

Robinson dominated the Middleweight division even when well into his thirties. He won the Championship five times, here seen against Carmen Basilio.

As champion, Robinson further indulged extravagant tastes and in order to account for back taxes (Joe Louis was ruined by a similar problem), he travelled to Europe. After knocking out Jean Stock in Paris on 27 November 1950, he fought in Brussels, Geneva, Paris again and finally in Frankfurt on Christmas Day, when he knocked out Hans Stretz.

On 14 February 1951 Robinson challenged La Motta for the middleweight championship. La Motta had held the title since June 1949, when he took it from Marcel Cerdan – an outstanding but ultimately tragic French-Algerian from Casablanca who, with his manger Jo Longman, was killed in an air crash *en route* to the United States for a return contest.

A crowd of 14,802 paid $180,619 to see Robinson and La Motta fight for the fifth and last time. Schoor described a predictably savage battle thus:

The best there ever was. Sugar Ray Robinson is lifted in triumph by his manager, Harold Johnson, after gaining a split decision over Carmen Basilio in Chicago on 25 March 1958.

> At the opening bell La Motta moved out as if he didn't care what happened to him. He carried the fight to Robinson, hoping to weaken him with an early body attack. Robinson came back strongly in the 2nd round with vicious hooks and right crosses to the champion's jaw. By the end of the 4th round Robinson seemed to be tiring and at the start of the 5th La Motta

CARMEN
BASILIO

charged out of his corner, cutting loose with everything he had. He hurt Robinson with blasting left hooks to the body and then shook him with a right that brought blood from his mouth. It was the Bull's best round.

Then the tide turned. Robinson snapped Jake's head back with a storm of punches. His jabs were like flashes of summer lightning, and the short rights to the jaw halted Jake in his tracks. Ray was in complete charge. In the 11th La Motta staged his final rally. For 30 seconds he threw every kind of punch but Robinson took most of them on his gloves. At the end of the 12th Gainford said, 'Now baby, this is the round. You got him. Turn him under. Throw them uppercuts, keep throwin' 'em.'

Robinson evoked a 64-day clause in his contract and regained the title on a technical knock-out in the tenth round in New York in September 1951. Badly cut in the ninth, Robinson might have lost again, had Turpin taken in a count, instead of attempting to withstand Robinson's desperate onslaught in the next round.

After 2 minutes 4 seconds of the thirteenth round, referee Frank Sykora stopped the contest. Robinson had taken La Motta apart.

Until June of that year, La Motta remained the only fighter who had defeated Robinson; then came an astonishing upset in London. Fascinated by Europe and to meet fresh tax demands, Robinson returned for another barnstorming tour and in little more than a month fought in Paris, Zurich, Antwerp, Liège, Berlin and Turin. He was not in the best of shape but Randolph Turpin, the British middleweight, did not appear to be a threat and Robinson accepted £28,000 to defend his championship in London, protecting himself with a 64-day return clause – a wise move in view of what occurred.

Robinson drew a huge crowd when he arrived in London with an entourage that included a valet, a barber, a golf professional and a midget jester. He drove a pink Cadillac and hotel porters were required to handle 53 suitcases. In contrast, Turpin came quietly to a contest that drew 18,000 to the Exhibition Hall at Earls Court; but an hour after going to his corner, the former Merchant Navy cook was

Randolph Turpin proved himself to be one of Britain's best ever boxers when taking the Middleweight Championship from Sugar Ray Robinson in London on 10 July 1951. The former Merchant Navy cook from Leamington Spa was given no chance against the greatest pound-for-pound fighter in boxing history, but won a clear points decision.

proclaimed middleweight champion of the world.

Robinson had seriously underestimated the British champion and knew that the return in New York on 12 September would not be a formality. By the tenth round, he was bleeding from a bad cut and it looked as though the younger man's strength might prove to be a decisive factor in the closing stages. Sensing this, Robinson suddenly cut loose. A terrible right sent Turpin down. He regained his feet and retreated to the ropes under heavy fire. With only eight seconds of the round remaining, referee Ruby Goldstein stepped between them; Robinson had regained the championship. Despite winning the British Empire light-heavyweight championship, Turpin was never the same man. He retired in 1958 and was found shot dead at his home in May 1966.

Robinson went on to win the 11 st 6 lb title a further three times. After successful defences against Bobo Olsen and Rocky Graziano and an abortive attempt to take the light-heavyweight championship from Joey Maxim, he first retired in 1952. He came back two years later and defeated Olsen in December 1955 to become champion again. He was nearly 34 years old.

Never as successful in business as he was in the ring, extravagant and profligate, Robinson, in common with so many great champions, fought on long past his time. He lost the championship to Gene Fullmer but regained it with a knock-out. When nearly 37, he took it back from Carmen Basilio.

A fortune had drained away and financial imperatives forced Robinson to continue boxing. At nearly 40, he lost the title to Paul Pender and lost again in the return. He fought on until his forty-fifth year. He died, aged 67, in April 1989.

Time waits for no fighter. Sugar Ray Robinson was 42 when he drew with Fabbio Bettini at the Palazzo dello Sport, Rome on 28 November 1964.

When the improbable journey began, Robinson claimed he would be different, that he could find a life after boxing, but in old age he became a sad figure, unable to comprehend the simplest messages reaching his confused mind.

It is the stubborn belief of people in boxing that Robinson's condition was entirely the result of a debilitating nervous disorder, but the blows he took come hurtling out of memory. Robinson's predicament evoked an overwhelming sense of melancholy, and was a reason to rage against boxing. ■

MUHAMMAD ALI

In a small room, referred to amusingly as my study, there is a large framed poster listing all but one of Muhammad Ali's 61 professional contests; each bout is represented by a glove. Ali won the heavyweight championship three times, a record, and those triumphs are celebrated in gold. The other gloves are coloured red. Within the square they form is a tale without equal in the history of boxing.

The poster was issued shortly before Ali, a month from his fortieth birthday, lost a unanimous decision over ten rounds to Trevor Berbick, the Canadian champion but little more than a heavy-armed swinger, in an appropriately shabby baseball stadium in the Bahamas on 11 December 1981. Where there had been turbulence there was only a muted awareness of extinction and, in increasingly slurred responses that hinted at a condition more serious than self-delusion, the chilling realization that the rest of Ali's life might become unbearably bleak.

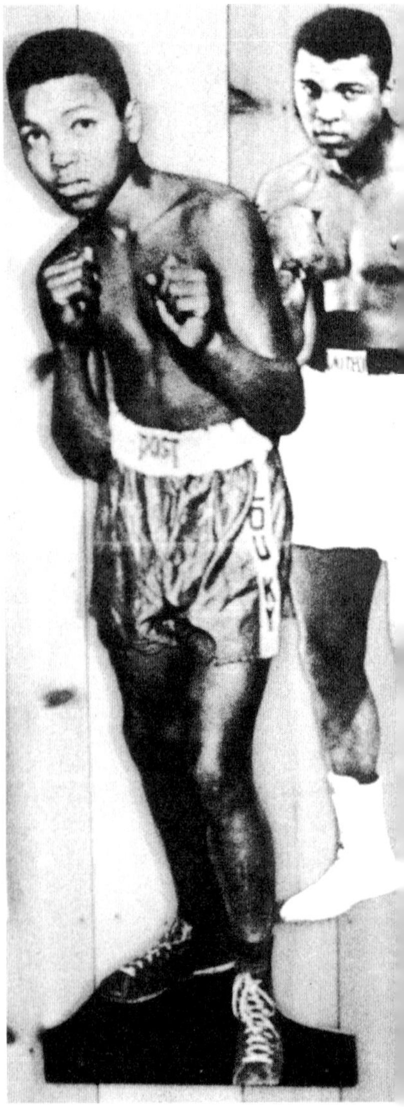

Ali was born Cassius Marcellus Clay II on 17 January 1942 in Louisville, Kentucky, the eldest son of an erratic, moderately successful sign-writer. The noble Roman names came from General Cassius Marcellus Clay, a benevolent, radical nineteenth-century plantation owner; the light skin from his mother, Odessa Grady, granddaughter of an Irish immigrant.

For the disenfranchized in our society, boxing, more than any other sport, represents a means of transcending fate, of refining and legitimizing the rage induced by deprivation and festering prejudice; an escape route from urban squalor as it became for Eddie Futch, a notable black trainer; recalling grim experiences shared with Joe Louis – perhaps the greatest of heavyweight champions – in an impoverished area of Detroit known explicitly as Black Bottom, he said: 'I remember being just 15 years old, looking in the mirror, wondering where the scar would be.

A wall of fame
From boy to man,
a career in retrospect

I used to wonder why I would go to jail. I knew I would go to jail for something. That is how it was.'

It is natural to assume that Ali sprang from similar circumstances, but, interestingly, he was not a fugitive from the ghetto and there is no evidence of corrupting influence or delinquent tendencies. Although aware of discrimination, the injustices imposed by white society, he grew up relatively secure in the most respectable of Louisville's three black sections. He would recall:

> I started boxing because I thought this was the fastest way for a black person to make it. I was not that bright and quick in school, couldn't be a football or basketball player because you have to go to college and get all kinds of degrees and pass examinations. A boxer can just go to the gym, jump around, turn professional, win a fight, get a break, and he is in the money, if he is good enough he makes more than ball players make all their lives.

By the time Ali became all things to all people – hero, traitor, scoundrel, zealot, bigot, philanderer, philosopher, rabble-rouser, prophet, but above all the most remarkable and charismatic sportsman the world has ever known – fantasy thrived in his mind, the vivid images frequently of cosmic proportions. For the majority, dreams dissolve in the acid of life; for the young Cassius Clay, they were the very essence of his being and seldom can a boy have known such a profound sense of destiny.

Angelo Dundee, the famed manager–trainer who was still in Ali's corner when the end came, remembers him first from a visit to Louisville with Willie Pastrano, a notable free-wheeler who won the light-heavyweight championship in 1963. 'The kid was only sixteen but there was something special about him even then,' Dundee said.

'Float like a butterfly, sting like a bee.' Drew 'Bundini' Brown (far right), self styled guru watches a young Ali on the scales while Angelo Dundee tries to muscle in.

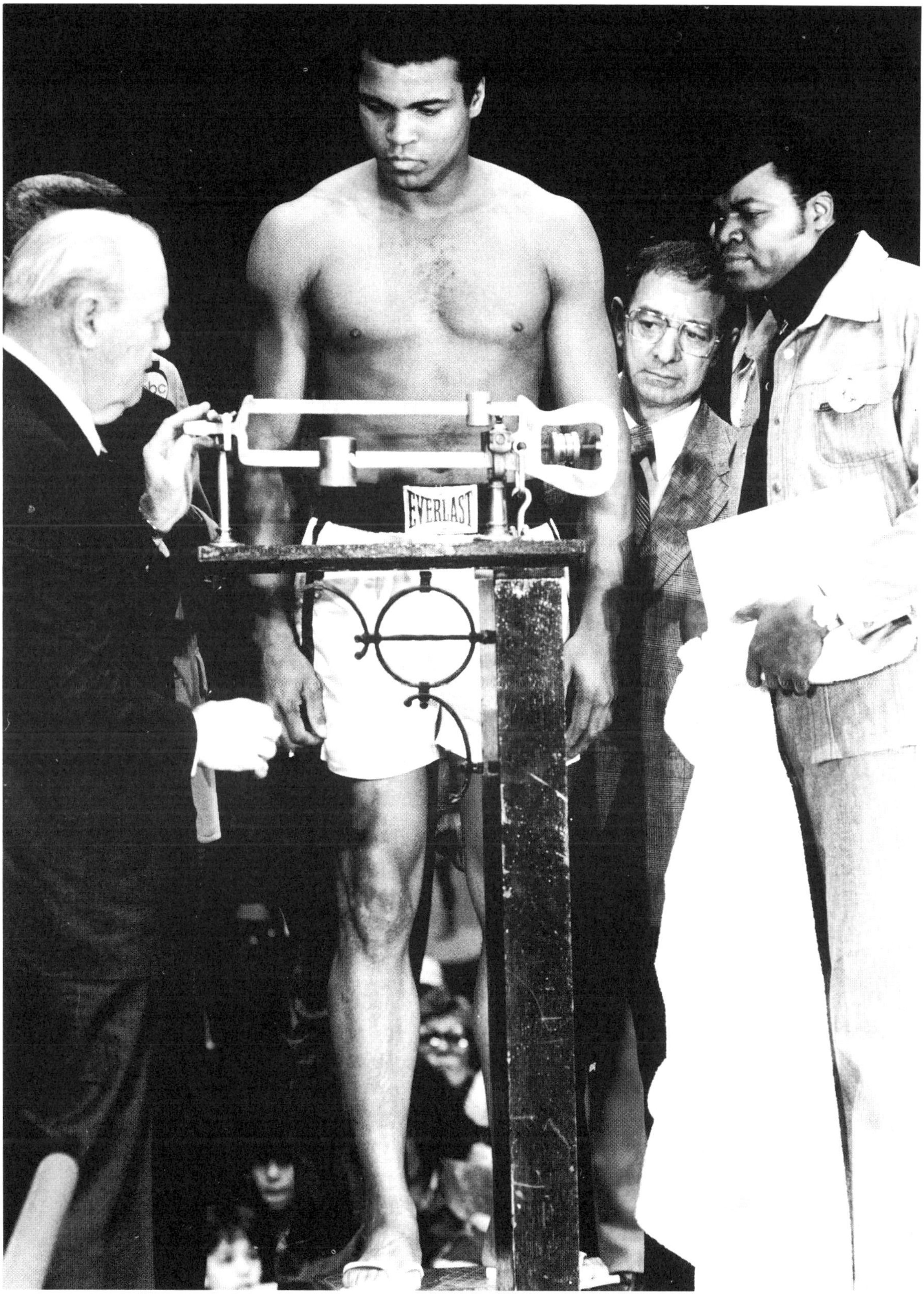
EVERLAST

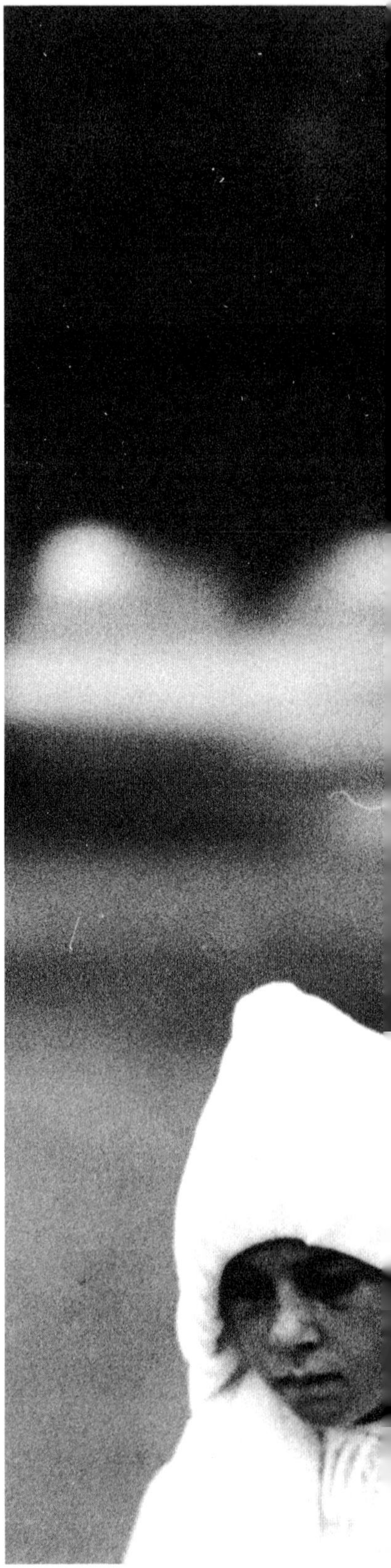

The heavyweight who was thought to be unbeatable. Sonny Liston in strange company, in training to defend the championship against Ali. Beaten twice by the young man from Louisville Kentucky, he was later found dead in Las Vegas.

'Something about the way he moved. Something about the way he talked. He's not only the most amazing fighter I've ever come across, he's the most unusual human being, the most fascinating person I've ever met.'

In July 1960, already established as an outstanding amateur, Clay arrived in Rome with the United States Olympic team. On 15 September, in the Palazzo dello Sport, he outpointed Zbigniew Piertrzkowski of Poland to win the light-heavyweight gold medal.

Clay returned to a civic reception in Louisville, but within days disenchantment had set in. Withered by humiliation after being refused service at a local hamburger restaurant, he went to a nearby river bridge and cast his Olympic medal into the water. It was then that he chose the roof of the world as a stage.

Until Clay embraced the Black Muslim faith in 1962, he was managed by the Louisville Group, a consortium of local business men formed to direct his affairs and invest his earnings. Their most important decision was to engage Angelo Dundee.

When Clay first arrived at Dundee's Fifth Street gym in Miami, the gnarled old pros shook their heads. In their terms he did everything wrong, obeying none of the tenets they held sacrosanct. He carried his hands low, by his hips, and instead of slipping punches he pulled away, swaying so far out of range that he often appeared to be hopelessly off balance. Fighters are taught to deliver blows from a solid base; Clay stayed on his toes, reaching always for the head, never the body, but in Dundee's mind a bad habit was only one that did not work. What he saw was a genius of the ring, a unique fighter possessing the hand and foot speed of a welterweight, the reflexes of a master swordsman, laser-beam accuracy, immense courage and a remarkable will. Mar-

'Body all tired and wracked with pain.' Ali at work in the Fifth Street gym in Miami.

velling at the astonishingly precise judgements Clay made, even under the heaviest fire, Dundee wisely confined himself to minor refinements and astute matchmaking.

The opponents he chose quickly discovered that Clay's extravagant style could be utterly bemusing and in their puzzled eyes and on their pummelled faces there was proof of emerging greatness. Heavyweights traditionally do not mature until their mid-twenties, so when Clay, at little more than five weeks past his twenty-second birthday, was matched with Sonny Liston for the championship on 25 February 1964 in Miami Beach, Florida, students of the noble art were entitled to suppose he was crucially short of experience.

What chance did a boy braggart, even one as comprehensively equipped as Clay appeared to be, have against a man whose brooding countenance fully complemented an awesome reputation? They were not to know that Clay, about to become Muhammad Ali, was also about to become a happening.

Red Smith, a distinguished American sports columnist described it thus: 'Cassius Marcellus Clay fought his way out of the horde that swarmed and leaped and shouted in the ring, climbed like a squirrel onto the red velvet ropes and brandished his still-gloved hand aloft. "Eat your words," he howled to the working press rows, "Eat your words."'

As the new champion, Clay was ready to confront America's White Establishment, to declare his blackness, to align himself with Islam and the most militant of civil rights movements then at work in the United States. Taking the name Muhammad Ali, he became a microcosm of his times and must be judged in that context. Black Society was on the march and who better to represent their cause than the most thrilling

MADISON SQ. GARDEN
TUES. SEPT. 15
MAIN EVENT
FLOYD
ALI

'The first time his ass hits the floor he'll bounce back up', said Angelo Dundee when asked about the extent of Muhammad Ali's will. Ali goes down from a left hook in the fourteenth round against Joe Frazier in their first fight at Madison Square Garden. True to his trainer's prediction, Ali regained his feet but lost a 15-round decision.

virtuoso boxing had ever seen. The Reverend Jesse Jackson has said: 'Ali did not legitimize the nation of Islam. He helped publicize it. Islam at that time was espousing a philosophy of self-determination and independence that made it different from the civil rights thrust. He went beyond the civil rights goal as an objective. Ali helped to internationalize black consciousness as much as anybody. People didn't turn to Islam because of Ali. They simply fought for his right to exercise his religious beliefs.'

To have been around Ali is to be aware of a sincere response to spiritual motivation, but those who saw him as evil incarnate reacted with predictable hostility when he refused to be drafted for Vietnam. That futile and ultimately debilitating conflict had yet to trouble America's conscience and though thousands of young men were fleeing the country, Ali was fined $10,000 and sentenced to five years' imprisonment. Within hours he was also stripped of his title by the New York Commission and the World Boxing Association. Ali appealed and there followed more than three years in exile until the Supreme Court at last ruled in his favour.

Hyperbole is a way of life in boxing; contests are always invested with dramatic consequence and fighters acquire sobriquets that usually suggest violence. Joe Louis was 'The Brown Bomber', Roberto Duran, 'Hands of Stone'. Ali's style was explicit in the words of his guru, Drew 'Bundini' Brown, 'float like a butterfly, sting like a bee', but he had no need of fancy appellation. It was enough to be 'Ali' and since his return to the ring coincided with an explosion in the telecommunications industry, he became the most conspicuous figure on earth.

The second phase of Ali's career was certainly the most momentous. He began to earn in multiples of seven figures and fought for the

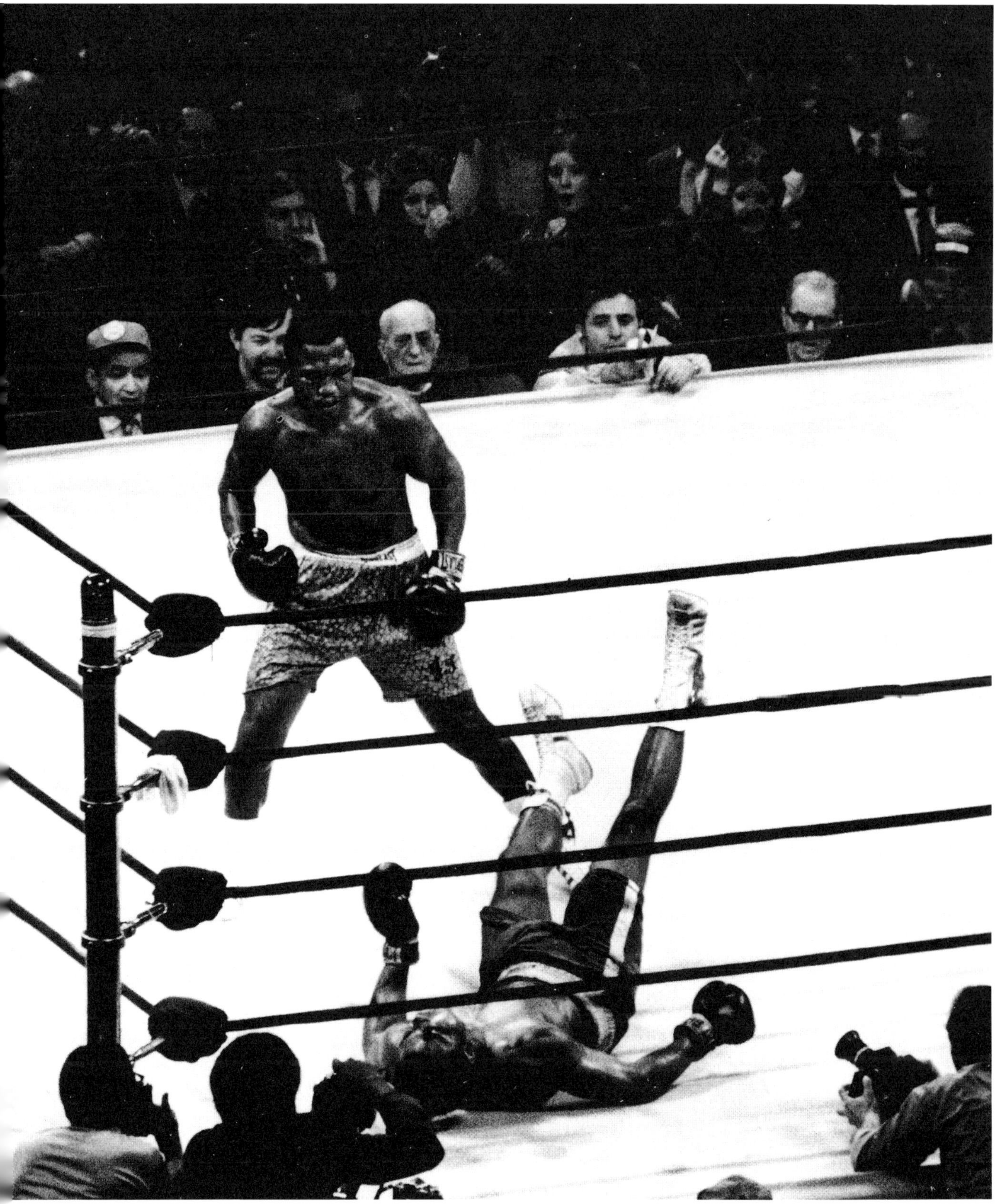

championship in bizarre locations. He took it from George Foreman in Zaïre and defended it, most thrillingly, against Joe Frazier, his great adversary, in Manila. In 1978 Ali rolled back the stone again when regaining the title from Leon Spinks in New Orleans.

However one looks at fame, Ali is famous and not merely for his prowess in the ring. People associate Ali with boxing in the way they associate Babe Ruth with baseball or Jack Nicklaus with golf. The connection thrives in their subconscious and is therefore a measure of true fame.

The headline tells it all. Ali nurses a swollen jaw after being outpointed by Joe Frazier.

He treads carefully now, each step a measure of the bleakness that inhabits his mind, but for almost two decades, from the moment he dethroned Sonny Liston to that miserable night in the Bahamas when the last rites were read over the most remarkable career in boxing history, Muhammad Ali held us in his spell.

It is no exaggeration to suggest that Ali was, and probably still is, one of the most famous men on the planet and even people who never miss an opportunity to boast that they are utterly uninformed about sport were in awe of his enormous talent for the most basic of physical contests.

Following Ali was almost a career in itself and a 14-year spell with the Sunday Mirror *provided opportunities to catch up with him when the volume had been turned down. Release from the constraints of daily journalism – that nagging awareness of deadlines – was important, as my friend Hugh McIlvanney of the* Observer *explained in his anthology on boxing: 'With him [Ali] the short sharp interview rarely elicited anything but a stage turn, a revamping of material that might or might not be entertaining but had almost certainly been heard before. By far the best bet was to try to merge in with his life for a day or two or at least for several hours at a stretch, simply to hang*

DAILY NEWS
JOE WINS
BY DECISION

around as unobtrusively as possible, eavesdropping on the strange meanderings of his spirit and just occasionally tossing in a few questions when he seemed susceptible to being nudged in directions that suited the eavesdropper.'

The confidence of people close to Ali was central to the application of that technique and we were constantly grateful for the assistance provided by his gregarious trainer, Angelo Dundee, and the two most loyal members of his entourage, Howard Bingham and Gene Kilroy. They led us into some strange dawns.

After returning from exile and the loss to Joe Frazier of the heavyweight championship in March 1971, Ali took part in 14 contests before the remarkable resurrection in Zaïre three years later. Because of his high profile, none could be ignored but they had to be evaluated in prospect and the meeting with Ken Norton, on 31 March 1973, did not appear to justify the expense of travelling to southern California. Although ranked seventh in the heavyweight division, Norton, a former US Marine, had not fought anyone who could be described as a serious contender for the championship and was thought to be another easy touch for Ali. This proved to be a wild miscalculation. Norton outpointed Ali and broke his jaw.

Styles are important to assessments in boxing and of all the men Ali went in with, the handsome Californian confused him most. Taking full advantage of long arms, Norton boxed at long range and employed spoiling tactics that were effective against all but the heaviest punchers. Despite two subsequent victories, Ali never mastered him or learned to avoid the overarm right that did so much damage in San Diego.

The reports that reached London in the early hours of 1 April 1973 suggested some attention should be paid to the date. Ali defeated by a comparative unknown, hospitalized with a broken jaw. It was the stuff of sensation and the Sunday papers reacted accordingly.

Within 24 hours there was plenty of evidence to support the suspicion that Ali had not prepared thoroughly for the contest and had reached a critical point in his career.

The X-rays showed a quarter-inch separation in the jaw-bone and surgeons expressed astonishment that he had fought for ten rounds with such an injury.

On the following Wednesday, I left for New York, hoping to get an audience with Ali at his home in Cherry Hill, New Jersey.

★ ★ ★ ★ ★

The assignment began with a telephone call to Angelo Dundee in Miami.

'No problem,' he piped. 'Get yourself over here and I'll sort out something. Call me when you arrive.'

The invitation sounded worryingly vague, but from experience Angelo was to be trusted, so it was with some confidence that I called him from Manhattan. Nothing. Dundee was not expected back at his office until the end of the week and could not be contacted at home. In desperation I tried his elder brother, Chris, a veteran, gravel-voiced fight promoter who more than adequately matches the stereotype.

'Don't know where Angelo is,' he growled, the words barely audible. A pause and then a glimmer of hope. 'I think he and Ferdie are going to see Ali tomorrow. They talked about flying to Philly in the morning. Best I can do for you.'

Ferdie Pacheco, now a boxing analyst with NBC, the American television network, was Ali's physician and also worked the corner with Angelo. Things were taking shape and early the next morning I set out to meet the first flight into Philadelphia from Miami.

It was barely light when I left the Algonquin Hotel on 44th Street,

A fighter's legs are his strength, his energy, his escape route. Ali builds up a rhythm in the Fifth Street gym Miami.

slumped in the back of an ancient cab, in no mood for conversation.

'Business?' ventured the driver, swerving violently to avoid a small crater in the road.

I grunted affirmation.

He tried again. 'Whaddya do?'

'Newspaperman,' I replied.

It seemed to impress him. 'Where ya from?'

'London.'

'Is that right. So what brings you here?'

It was a mistake, but I told him and he laughed.

'The guy had it coming,' he said. 'Norton shut his big mouth.'

Taking the Mid-Town Tunnel, he got me quickly to La Guardia Airport. I glanced at the ID clipped to the dashboard. Verecchi. Paulo Verecchi.

On the short flight pessimism broke out again, sour as the coffee that came in a paper cup. Perhaps Dundee had altered the arrangements or aborted the trip.

Four hours later, there was still no sign of them and I was beginning to get desperate. They arrived on the next flight. Pacheco looked surprised when he saw me.

'Were you expecting this guy to be here?' he asked Dundee who had clearly not mentioned our arrangement. My heart dropped. Dundee smiled away an obvious dilemma.

'Sure I did,' he said, too shrewd to admit he had forgotten. 'Howya doin' Kenny?'

A short man wearing a blue raincoat moved towards us. 'Meet my brother Jimmy,' said Dundee. 'He's driving us out to see my guy.' It was the way Dundee liked to speak of Ali, although everybody in boxing

SQ. GARDEN
FLOYD
VS.
GREEN

knew he merely supervised training and ran the corner, a subordinate to Herbert Muhammad, son of Elijah Muhammad, the leader of the Black Muslims – a movement to which Ali had made a substantial commitment.

Jimmy Dundee, who worked for the American Government until his death a few years ago, steered out of the airport and deftly on to the freeway, moving from behind a large truck and into the fast lane. The manoeuvre completed, he asked his brother to elaborate on what had occurred so dramatically in San Diego.

'My guy hurt Norton in the second round and then, pop, over comes a right, bang on the whiskers,' Angelo chirped. 'Right away I knew something was wrong and when he got back to the corner, we knew the jaw was broken.'

Two troublesome back teeth had been removed from Ali's mouth a week or so prior to the contest and Dundee suspected that the injury resulted from a temporary weakness in the jaw-bone. Whatever the reason, Ali, by then 31 years old, could no longer afford to ignore the ravages of time or the disciplines without which he could not hope to achieve maximum fitness.

'He ain't a kid no more,' Dundee said, 'and those marvellous legs ain't coming back. But once all this is over, he's got to do some work.'

Jimmy Dundee turned the car into a half-made road and stopped outside a large house that stood off to the right. Gene Kilroy was waiting and he crossed the lawn to greet Angelo and Ferdie. Seeing me, he gave them a puzzled glance.

'Who the hell is this?' he asked. One of the few white men to gain Ali's confidence, Kilroy, a burly Irish-American, was best described by Gary Smith in a notable *Sports Illustrated* feature that brought a famous

Nobody gave Ken Norton much chance against Ali when they fought for the first time in San Diego on 31 March, 1973, but the ex-marine broke the former champion's jaw and won a 12-round decision.

EVERLAST

entourage, the extravagent Ali circus, back to life:

Gene Kilroy had no title. Everyone just knew: He was the Facilitator. When Ali wanted a new Rolls-Royce, Kilroy facilitated it. When he wanted land to build a training camp, Kilroy facilitated it. When a pipe burst in the training camp or a hose burst in the Rolls, when Marlon Brando or Liza Minelli wanted to meet Ali, or Ali wanted to donate $100,000 to save an old-folk's home, Kilroy facilitated it.

I came to know Kilroy well, but that first meeting was tense.

'For Chrisake Angelo, you know we agreed to keep a low profile. No interviews until the man gets his mouth working properly again.' Dundee looked sheepish.

I followed them into a low structure that cloistered a large garden and waited for a decision.

After a while, Kilroy indicated that I was welcome. 'The man is in there,' he said, nodding in the direction of what turned out to be a small study. Ali sat behind a desk clutching a crimson telephone; scissors poked from the breast pocket of a black shirt, carried to cut through the wire that bound his jaw because there was a danger that he could choke on vomit. Ali greeted me with his eyes and glanced across at Dundee.

'We'll speak on the way in to town,' he mumbled.

I imagined it would be necessary to suffer familiar routines, flights of outrageous fancy, ludicrous prophecies and wearying Black Muslim sermons, but Ali proved to be unusually serious, showing no inclination to diminish the extent of his set-back.

'I've been punished,' he said, grinding out the words over his immobilized jaw. Punished for what? Taking opponents too lightly? For

Main picture: Ali admired Joe Frazier for coming on through the jabs. He felt less generous when taking this powerful right to the side of his jaw, a blow that also had some effect on Drew 'Bundini' Brown who can be seen waving excitedly in Ali's corner.

'We're just brothers makin' a livin', Ali said of his three memorable contests with Joe Frazier. They should have both retired from the ring after a punishing encounter in Manila in 1975.

A bad habit is only a bad habit if it doesn't work, top right. Muhammad Ali defied the accepted tenets of boxing, here pulling away from rather than slipping inside the arc of Joe Frazier's left hook.

squandering the great gift. 'I've been punished,' he repeated, the refusal to elaborate an admission that he had not been in the best condition since losing to Frazier two years earlier.

On the way to a medical in Philadelphia, he removed both hands from the wheel of a dark blue Rolls, the flurry of fake punches that followed drawing an instant rebuke from Dundee. 'Angelo, you think I'm finished?' he asked. 'Some guy on the telephone said you thought I was.'

Dundee winced. 'Look, this newsman stops me on the way out of the ring and asks me if you are through. What kind of a damn question was that. They twist things around.'

'This guy needs a challenge,' said Pacheco.

'You're right,' said Ali. 'They said that Liston was unbeatable. I beat him. They said I couldn't become the person I wanted to be. I became that person. They said I couldn't come back. I came back. Now they say I'm finished. I'll prove that I'm not.'

Emerging from four days of morose silence, Ali attempted to rationalize a miserable experience. 'I felt it go,' he said. 'A crack. I could move the jaw-bone around with my glove. From then on it wasn't about winning any more. I had to finish the fight.' Thinking about it encouraged him to employ some ritual bragging. 'If there is a next time, they will have to stop it. Norton has no right to be in the same ring as men. Who is Ken Norton? I don't hear about people beating down his door. I don't see him on no TV shows. The trouble is that I'm not supposed to lose. But what's a broken jaw? Your leg is broken. Get up and walk. I'm easier to get at. People look for signs. Ali's lost his speed. His legs have gone. His hands are no longer fast. They can hit him now. But how many great fighters never lost? Joe Louis, Ray Robinson. They

'I kept thinking about what a great father Joe is, how much he loves his kids. I didn't want him to end up a cabbage.' Frazier reels from one of the blows that persuaded trainer Eddie Futch to retire him at the end of the fourteenth round.

lost. Liston lost. But when Ali loses, it is like an earthquake.'

Pacheco reckoned it would be six weeks before Ali could think about returning to the gym, but he was confident that Ali would make a complete recovery. There was also the possibility that painful defeat had provided him with necessary stimulus.

'The guy's hurting,' Dundee said as we sat waiting for the latest verdict. 'He knows this is a crisis in his life. Of course he's lost some of that phenomenal leg speed. But when has he ever danced around as he did against Liston? A lot of it has been an illusion.'

An illusion? I thought about that on a train back to New York and again the next morning on my way to the *Mirror* bureau in Manhattan. It was early and just about light as I walked down towards 3rd Avenue, cutting through Grand Central Station and on towards the East River. Perhaps it was all an illusion.

Only in America. Don King, the flamboyant American promoter and former numbers racketeer, congratulates Tim Witherspoon who retained the World Boxing Association Heavyweight Championship when he stopped Frank Bruno in the eleventh round at Wembley on 19 July 1986.

So to Africa; the dark continent, jungle Africa. So to Zaïre, where, on 30 October 1974, Muhammad Ali staged his resurrection: knocking out George Foreman in the eighth round – the most bizarre and dramatic event boxing has ever known.

It began to take form six months earlier in Caracas, Venezuela, the day after George Foreman crushed Ken Norton: a victory achieved with such chilling certainty that it no longer seemed an exaggeration to think of the Texan as a uniquely destructive force in the division.

Foreman versus Ali was a natural progression but, to our astonishment, it would take place in Kinshasa, Zaïre, drawn together by Don King, the black entrepreneur from Cleveland who had begun to emerge as a significant presence in boxing.

When King speaks, it is with the absolute confidence of a man who learned

Ali had to take heavy punishment in Zaïre, wincing here as Foreman closes in to deliver a thunderous hook to the lower ribs.

the value of outrageous communication somewhere along the way from the numbers racket he operated in Cleveland to prison to a racket known otherwise as boxing promotion. He served 3 years 11 months at the Marion Correctional Institute in Ohio before being paroled in September 1971. He was convicted of second-degree murder, later reduced to manslaughter, after beating to death a man who owed him money. In 1954 he shot and killed a man caught robbing a house which was used as a collection point. The judge ruled justifiable homicide. King was eventually pardoned in January 1983, two years after being honoured as one of Cleveland's outstanding native sons.

King at full blast, outbursts of strident hyperbole interspersed with detonations of manic laughter, employed a considerable gift to persuade all inhabitants of the universe that the coming together of Foreman and Ali was an event of symbolic proportions. 'The prodigal sons will be returning home to Africa,' he declared. 'This will be a spectacular such has never yet been staged on earth.'

The consortium involved in the contest included Risnelia Investment (a Panamanian group that had links with the Zaïre Government). Hemdale Leisure Corporation (a British company), Video Techniques Incorporated of New York and Don King Productions. It would take place at 3 a.m. in the Stadium of the Twentieth of May, with world-wide viewing figures estimated at more than a billion.

★ ★ ★ ★ ★

We had gathered in a bungalow set alongside the verdant expanse of the Zaïre River. There was an overwhelming sense of anxiety because the fight was only a few hours away and most of us feared for Muhammad Ali.

What a strange time it had been. First the postponement: the

unavoidable impression that Bill McMurray, an obscure part-time sparring partner in the Foreman camp, had contributed mightily to Ali's downfall by cutting his employer's right eye – the injury bringing about a six weeks' delay that many believed would disturb the delicate balance of the challenger's preparation. Boredom; a steady deterioration of will, out at N'Sele, 40 miles from Kinshasa, all things were mysterious. A government complex of some 1,000 acres, stretching 2 miles inland from river bank to highway, everywhere the numinous presence of President Mobutu. Mobutu Sese Seko Kuku Ngbendu Wa Za. Banga – 'all powerful warrior who, because of his endurance and inflexible will to win, will go from conquest to conquest leaving fire in his wake'.

'I done kicked a lotta butts, all them people who thought George was the baddest man in the world,' triumphed Muhammad Ali after knocking out George Foreman to regain the Heavyweight Championship in Zaïre in 30 October 1974.

For the hundreds of media representatives who had flown in from the United States and Europe, a week at N'Sele was more than enough and as we set off for home that first time, many vowed not to return, the Americans in particular expressing despair with Zaïre's attempt to stage an event of such magnitude; telephones that never rang, teleprinters that stood as lifeless decorations in the Press room. Ludicrous censorshp. 'If I come back, I'm bringing a crate of pigeons and a set of semaphore flags,' snapped one irate writer from New York as he left for the airport.

What had been planned as a triumphant manifestation of Ziare's potential was in danger of collapse as Ali's physician, Ferdie Pacheco, recalled in his book *Fight Doctor*:

The weeks prior to fight week had just about seen the sinking of the Don King flagship on the troubled waters of the fight game. First, his promised avalanche of tourists had not materialized. And a fortunate thing it was, too, since it turned out to be the rip-off of the decade. Monies were paid in

the States, but no one in Kinshasa got the message so that the promised and paid-for hotel rooms were not available, and the rest of the goodies were not to be had. Lawsuits were flying. Next, a poster idea went down like a Belgian hot dog, the slogan being senseless and offensive to native Africans: From Slaveship to Championship. Huge posters were printed bearing this headline. Africans stared uncomprehendingly at the slogan. After all, Africans are the ones who stayed and *sent* the slaves: they were the slave traders, not the slaves, and they could not relate to the message in the sense that American blacks can relate.

When making his first public appearance since the accident, emerging from the heavily guarded compound he shared with his entourage and a German police dog, Foreman's vague responses were sufficient to evoke suspicion 'I will decide when the eye is ready,' he growled. 'I am my own doctor.'

A month later, we were back in Zaïre. This time we were given a choice: either N'Sele, barely edible meals supplemented by daily raids on Angelo Dundee's refrigerator, but close proximity to Ali; or more comfortable accommodation in Kinshasa. Together with Hugh McIlvanney of the *Observer*, I settled for N'Sele.

Making some sense of it was not easy amid the shrillness that surrounded the challenger. Soaring from one fanciful proclamation to another, Ali was in splendid form, but bleak images were gathering in the minds of those who had acquired an identity at his side, their strident optimism carrying little conviction. Darkness brought a shudder of doubt to them all, an awareness that their future hinged on the extent of Ali's will when exposed to Foreman's heavy artillery.

Ali talked of how he would react if the champion knocked him down. 'I'll be jabbin' and dancin' till my head clears again. I'll run, I'll rassle. I

'Holmes and Tate and all the rest gotta know I'm still the best.' Muhammad Ali holds court before losing to Holmes in Las Vegas.

won't be giving George no target, but shit, he ain't goin' to get to me. I'm not gonna be there,' he said rising from a settee in his bungalow to demonstrate the techniques of survival, dancing around the room, miming retaliatory flurries.

In a quieter mood, he studied a video of Foreman training 'How can I lose to someone that clumsy, that ugly?' he declared scathingly. Crowds gathered daily; excited children, silent woman with more than admiration ablaze in their eyes. And always the chant; *Ali, boom-ah-yay, Ali, knock him down and kill him.* Ali orchestrated from the ring, a hand waved in unison with the syllables.

Down by the river, grateful for Dundee's hospitality, we attempted to arrive at an objective conclusion, unashamedly responsive to suggestions that Foreman would be found out if the fight progressed beyond half-way. 'If George don't get me in seven, his parachute won't open,' Ali had said a few weeks earlier. Dundee was quick to pounce on this, citing the evidence of two contests against Gregorio Peralta, a light-heavyweight who had twice taken the champion ten rounds, the first time to a decision.

'George is no monster,' he piped, 'and he's going to find out about his limitations.'

The lecture that followed had Dundee posturing a comic impersonation of Foreman's ponderous style. 'He wants to pull you on to punches or shove you away to a convenient range, but he won't be able to do that with my guy,' he insisted. 'If you go at George on a straight line, as Joe Frazier did, he will tear your head off. If you retreat on a straight line, he will tear you apart with those big swings. But give George angles and you give him trouble. Ali will be either inside or outside the arc of the heavy stuff and all the time his jab will be rattling into George's face. Muhammad will knock him out.'

None of this could completely allay our fears, not merely that Ali would be defeated but that he would be pulverized, the legend in ruins at Foreman's feet.

With the fight only a few hours away, there was no guarantee that we would make it to the ringside, our anxiety over this matter increasing with each minute spent in a room at the Memling Hotel in Kinshasa, waiting for the credentials to arrive, a scene described by Norman Mailer in *The Fight*:

> Once assembled, the reporters were kept waiting in the Press Room for an hour and a half. From seven in the evening to eight-thirty, two hundred members of the Press jammed a room whose fire laws would have closed the door at population eighty, and in the wan light of the fluorescent tubes, reporters were crowded in on one another like a fast growing culture in a Petri dish. Who knows the murderous remarks of bacteria? The media men talked with passion of Mobutu's lack of faculty for public relations, yet no one dared to leave. The Press representative, Tshimpumpu, had announced that he wished to speak to the Press. From experience, everyone knew the speech could contain information essential for getting into the stadium, mention of some arcane gate, for example, not listed on the ticket, but crucial. Besides, it was dangerous to miss picking up one's ticket. The rest of the night could be spent pleading with Tshimpumpu's assistants, who would be unable to make a decision without him. God's blood, one didn't want to miss obtaining the ticket now.

Tshimpumpu was known to some of us as a result of his extraordinary behaviour in West Germany a short while earlier. When reporting the

The truth shows in Muhammad Ali's eyes as he rests between rounds against Larry Holmes.

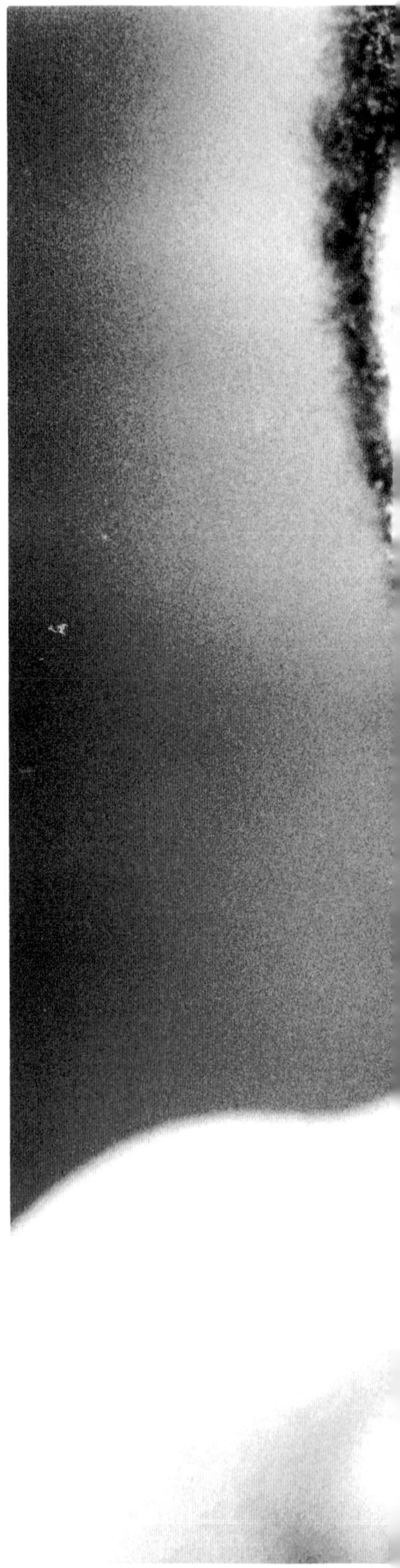

matches Zaïre played in the 1974 World Cup, he had sent a telex message of monumental length and embellished the legend by instructing a taxi driver to drive him 250 miles to Berlin. Now we were at his mercy. Tshimpumpu never arrived, leaving us to deal with Murray Goodman, a veteran New York publicist who solved the problem with a minimum of fuss, but not before one British writer of nervous disposition was driven to the brink of apoplexy.

Sport provides us with a convenient vehicle for exaggeration, success and failure, youth and ageing; when set against the ultimate verity, it is never thus and yet the drama that unfolded in the stadium of the twentieth of May was almost suffocatingly intense. Even before the fighters reached their corners, I trembled with anticipation, objectivity set aside, the committment to Ali absolute.

Of course, as long as there was life in his legs, he would dance, stick and move; taunt, parry, hold. Astonishingly, he retreated to the ropes, taking station half-way between his own and a neutral corner. An incredulous silence settled over the ringside. Foreman, at first puzzled, prowled forward and unleashed a wide hook to the body; then another. 'He's going to get killed,' yelled somebody in the row behind. Dundee and Drew 'Bundini' Brown led the chorus from Ali's corner, anxiety in every vowel. 'Move, for Christ sake move.' Ali did not move. He swayed back over the top rope, head angled out over the ring apron as Foreman closed with him again. Then a stinging combination of straight punches leaped into the champion's face.

The pattern did not alter through rounds two and three and Ali could be seen taunting Foreman: 'you got 12 more rounds of this sucker.' The champion made a big effort, in the fifth and a terrible left hook pounded into Ali's head; then another. The challenger stayed on his feet, hands

quickly in position so that he could retaliate with sharp counters. In the seventh, Ali moved forward for almost the first time in the contest, as though satisfied that he had drawn the last of the ogre's strength. Jabs began to jump into Foreman's face and a right almost sent him through the ropes.

At the start of the eighth, Foreman hit Ali with three punches to the head and then stumbled on to two rights. Sent sideways by a vicious left hook, he went down from the following right. Foreman rolled over and looked despairingly towards his corner – Dick Sadler, Archie Moore, Sandy Saddler. Not a head was to be seen. He struggled upright, but it was all over. Jack Clayton had completed the count.

Pandemonium. Upturned benches, a mad scramble to reach the dressing-rooms, a man prostrate beneath an ancient switchboard that was incongruously linked with a communications satellite. I hauled him up. It was a tearful Budd Schulberg, not in pain but consumed by joy. We fought our way through the crowds and I flopped down alongside Pacheco in Ali's dressing-room, our backs against a bare wall, observing an amazing scene. Pacheco nodded towards where Ali lay naked and still on a narrow padded table. 'They've already taken all his stuff,' he said, despairingly. 'His robe, his shorts, his gloves, his protector, his socks. They'll sell them.'

Then the rain came. The fight would not have survived such a downpour; one that turned the highway into a torrent, hammering on the roof of the springless vehicle that carried us back to N'Sele, the water level rising steadily up over the wheels. Our driver wanted none of it, pleading that it was impossible to complete the journey. We urged him on with promises.

Dawn and all was still at N'Sele, steam rising from the swollen river, giving ghostly form to the floating clumps of foliage so that they passed by like bloated carcasses. After a while, Hugh McIlvanney and I made our way towards Dundee's bungalow and suddenly Ali was standing in front of us. 'You want to speak to me?' he asked. We nodded, thrilled by the prospect of intimate conversation, and followed him into the villa. He lay back on a settee, legs stretched on to a low table. 'I kicked a lot of asses – not only George's,' he said contentedly. There was a slight redness in the corner of his right eye and the suspicion of a small bruise beneath it, but apart from those minor blemishes he was unmarked. 'All those writers who said I was washed up, all those people who thought I had nothing left but my mouth, all them who were waiting for me to get the biggest beatin' of all times: they thought George could do it for them, but they know better now.'

It became clear that Ali had long since sensed important deficiencies in Foreman, most importantly that hurt would be a new experience for him. 'Joe Frazier came on through the jabs, took them and kept coming. But did you see how George turned his head? He's not used to being hit and he needs room to hit you. I was nervous but not afraid because nothing new could happen to me. I had been knocked down and I had got up. I had lost fights and I had been stunned by big punches. George didn't know none of those things. I called him a sucker when he hit me good and asked him if that was the best he had.'

Ali closed his eyes. 'Nobody expected this,' he muttered, 'nobody. Muhammed Ali stops George Foreman. Man that's something a hell of an upset. I fooled them all.'

At 32 he was the champion again. ■

MUHAMMAD ALI

Time waits for no fighter. Ali, in the autumn of his career, sweats off surplus weight before defeating Leon Spinks in New Orleans in 1980, so becoming the first man to win the Heavyweight Championship three times. Opposite, Ali at his peak of fitness.

GEORGE FOREMAN

It was not necessary to invent a nom de guerre *for George Foreman, the huge and brooding Texan who threw the heavyweight championship into disarray in Kingston, Jamaica, on 22 January 1973, when he knocked out Joe Frazier after 95 seconds of the second round.*

Larger men have fought in the division, but Foreman conveyed such an awesome impression of brute force when sending the previously unbeaten champion down six times (one pulverizing right hurled Frazier so violently sideways that his feet left the canvas), that only a violently demoralizing experience could be imagined for anybody coming out of the opposite corner – including Muhammad Ali, who appeared to be in decline, his career by then at a low ebb.

This turned out to be a serious miscalculation, but until Ali's dramatic intervention almost two years later, Foreman, a gold medallist at the Mexico Games in 1968, was thought to be invincible, so intimidatingly powerful that comparisons were drawn with the great champions in history.

Born in Marshall, Texas, on 10 January 1949, the fifth of seven children, his father a construction worker, Foreman dropped out of high school at 14 and was considered to be a potentially dangerous delinquent before he enlisted in the Job Corps, the community welfare organization that rescued him from the Fifth Ward ghetto and assigned him to a centre in Pleasanton, California, about 40 miles east of Oakland.

He was persuaded to take up boxing by Nick 'Doc' Broadus, a Job Corps administrator and he fought for the first time in January 1967, winning by a knock-out. Within a year Foreman was the Golden Gloves and national amateur champion. He turned professional after winning the Olympic title and went to his corner in Kingston with an unblemished record: 37 victories, 34 inside the distance.

★ ★ ★ ★ ★

Almost everybody believed Joe Frazier would have too much for George Foreman. Some felt it would end quickly; others that it would last, only for as long as it took Frazier to draw the challenger's strength. Nobody expected it to go the distance.

Predicting the outcome of fights is still a long way from being a precise science, but we should have listened and paid some attention to the view being aired by two veteran observers of the sport, Bob Waters, who wrote with great distinction for *Newsday*, and Walter Bartleman, a much respected and greatly admired representative of the London *Evening Standard*. They both argued a case for Foreman.

'I'm looking at strength, size and ambition,' Waters said, 'and the possibility that Frazier is underestimating this guy. Then there is Joe's style. He fights the Philadelphia way, pressing forward, throwing hooks like he did against Ali and that will suit George.'

'I can't tell no jokes, I don't write no poems, but I'm the best in the world at knocking people down.' George Foreman before defending the World Heavyweight Championship against Ken Norton in Caracas, Venezuela.

'I'm the best in the world at knocking people down.' George Foreman ends Joe Frazier's reign as heavyweight champion. Kingston Jamaica 23 January 1973.

None of this impressed Frazier: 'George keeps saying he's going to do this and that. Smoke me out, cut me off at the gulch. All that stuff. I don't know how he intends to fight but he won't have any trouble finding me. I'm going to be up against his chest.'

We were sitting in a ground-floor hotel suite that looked out on a crowded swimming pool. It was about eleven o'clock in the morning. Frazier had on white linen slacks and a blue sweat-shirt and he was lounging on the bed, hands clasped loosely behind his head. Every now and then he tugged at the small beard that tufted from a belligerent chin. 'They say they'll let us know,' said Frazier's manager, Yank Durham, mysteriously, after replacing the telephone.

Frazier grunted and ran his fingers across dry lips, moistening them with his tongue and then reaching out for a glass of water. 'I'm nearly down to my best weight,' he said. 'I want to be around two hundred and eight. It wouldn't bother Yank if I came in as I am now, two fourteen or so. But I want to be a shade lighter because I want to be fast.'

Since outpointing Ali at Madison Square Garden on 8 March 1971, Frazier had twice defended the championship, easily defeating Terry Daniels and Ron Stander, two grossly over-matched challengers, while negotiations proceeded for a re-match that was being spoken of as the richest fight in history.

An awareness of this made it even more difficult to understand why Frazier had agreed to put his title at risk against an opponent who, although comparatively inexperienced, gave the impression that he could demolish a derelict buliding with one blow. 'I'm doing it for the money,' he said. 'It's that simple.'

As Frazier had been spending more time on the road with his pop group, The Knockouts, than in a gymnasium in Philadelphia notable for the sort of activity that intensifies the pressure imposed on casualty wards, Foreman was encouraged to believe that he was about to embarrass the odds makers who had installed the champion as a clear favourite. 'The way I see it, Joe can't get himself there any more,' Foreman said, 'Champions don't last for ever and it's time for him to go. It's different for me because there is still something I haven't done. But what has Frazier left to do? How many times do you keep going back to the gym when there is nothing left to prove?'

Large audiences gathered at Foreman's training sessions and, sensing an enthusiastic response, he made much of his strength, threatening to remove the heavy bag from its mooring with flat disembowelling hooks thrown from the hip, evoking expressions of mock horror in his manager–trainer, Dick Sadler, a small, round, extremely black man who needed little persuasion to break into the song and dance routines of his youth. 'Hey,

Frazier was down five times before Foreman knocked him out after 95 seconds of the second round.

hey. Nobody hits like my man,' he screeched. 'When he hits Frazier they can forget about the count because this boy is special. He punches like Sonny Liston used to and he moves good. Some fighters rely on speed. That's Ali. Others have to get hit before they can hit. That's Frazier. George don't depend on any one thing. But man, his power, that's special.'

The fight lasted only 4 minutes and 35 seconds, becoming quickly calamitous for Frazier, who was sent down three times in the opening round, his senses in a dishevilled state from the moment Foreman delivered a savage concussive right that landed before the champion's seconds had taken up position at the foot of the steps.

Few could claim to have witnessed similar proportions of ferocity and suddenness in the ring. Frazier remained dazed more than an hour after the referee, Arthur Mercante, stopped the contest, his co-ordination still in such obvious disarray that he found it difficult to tie his shoe-laces and fasten the buttons of a blood-red shirt. Foreman had prospered beyond all prediction, taking dramatic, killing advantage of the champion's almost suicidal eagerness to try to out-hit a bigger man. 'He punches faster than I thought he could,' Frazier mumbled. 'After that first knockdown I should have got on the move. With all that muscle, George might have been struggling after five or six rounds.'

The assessment would be crucial to Muhammad Ali's strategy in Zaïre, but there was no doubt that Frazier had fought like a novice, the outcome so sensational that rumours were inevitable.

It was suggested that Foreman had been training in private; that his ponderous public sessions were merely a disguise; that Frazier's reluctance to complete negotiations for a re-match with Ali in California stemmed from a fear of failing the stringent medical standards in that state.

A cook who had been with Frazier for five years was sacked on the eve of the contest and the confused circumstances of the champion's preparation were emphasized when he weighed in seven pounds more than was expected. Even Foreman's calm acceptance of a major triumph lent credibility to the suggestion that Frazier was in trouble from the moment he agreed to the defence. The whole thing was surreal, as though someone had made an awful mistake.

Why were Foreman's attendants, including Archie Moore and Sandy Saddler, two of the finest champions in history, so confident when the odds were heavily against their man? Bookmakers paid out in the National Stadium, but only small money and there was nowhere on the island where a sizeable bet could be struck.

The heavyweight championship had passed into the hands of a comparative if powerful novice and further confusion erupted two months later when Ken Norton broke Ali's jaw and outpointed him in San Diego.

A week before they came together again, in San Diego on 21 September, Foreman, his career on hold, took an easy defence against Joe 'King' Roman in Tokyo. With the advantage of an 11-hour time difference I sent this report to the *Sunday Mirror*:

Professional boxing suffered here as much from George Foreman's reckless, licensed abuse of its rules as it did from the lunacy of matching him with a barely adequate challenger.

There was always a serious doubt about whether Joe Roman had any right in the same ring as the man whose devastating power tore the undisputed world heavyweight title from Joe Frazier in Jamaica eight months ago.

Foreman, cold-eyed and merciless, took fewer than two minutes to confirm that. By then the Puerto Rican lay senseless at the champion's feet, overwhelmed by an onslaught of murderous blows.

But before the final barrage, Foreman so blatantly infringed the rules that had the fight been held in Europe, he would surely have been disqualified, losing his title on a foul.

Roman, stalked and cut off in that triangle of the ring apexed by his own corner, tried to escape along the ropes, only to find himself pinned down, ducking lower and lower beneath a relentless barrage of punches, most of which defied technical description. He went down with his back against the bottom strand, one foot still planted, the other twisted grotesquely sideways. Instead of stepping clear as the referee, Jay Edson, scurried in to begin the count, Foreman, taking deliberate aim, sent a clubbing right into the side of Roman's head.

There was instant pandemonium. Roman's ancient manager, Bill Daly, and his chief second, Al Braverman, leaped onto the ring apron and protested. Foreman fled, realizing the extent of his impetuosity, but sensation did not figure in Edson's estimate. He allowed Roman 30 seconds in which to recover and then committed him to destruction.

The rest was a formality. Roman went down again as Foreman, regaining some credit, shortened and corrected his punches, ending the fight with a brutal right uppercut after the challenger had taken a mandatory eight count. Then the acrimony.

When Foreman crossed the ring to commiserate with Roman, he was dismissed obscenely by the irate Braverman who then communicated his loathing to the reporters at ringside. 'That guy is disgusting,' he bellowed, the knuckles of his right hand white along the top rope. 'He's the heavyweight champion of the world but he behaved like street fighter. We don't need no handshake.' This was rich coming from an old reprobate who repeatedly gave the impression that he thought the Marquis of Queensbury to have been a meddling old fool. But he wasn't finished. 'If this fight had been in Europe, they'd have taken the title away from Foreman. The least we should have got was a couple of minutes to recover.'

Oblivious to the familiar royal reference, Roman was in no state to endorse the complaint as Dick Sadler, the champion's manager, mimed his own preposterous version of the incident.

Sadler, prone and balancing his right shoulder on the bottom rope, claimed that Roman hadn't reached the canvas when he was struck. Edson's ludicrous view, utterly invalidated by the television playback, was that it had been a reflex blow. The dispute continued in the dressing rooms though Daly's insistence that there would be a formal protest did not carry much conviction.

He knew what we all knew. That it was over and done with, consigned to history. Foreman who was jeered by the Japanese, at least admitted to a gross error of judgement. 'I made a mistake,' he said, 'and I agree Roman should have been given more time to recover. But if he wants to come back in 30 days I'll accommodate him.'

That is about as likely as it is that Foreman will be stripped of the championship.

A thrilling rally in the last round got Ali home on a split decision against Norton in Los Angeles, but it was the Californian who next challenged for the championship, taking his chance six weeks after Ali outpointed Frazier at Madison Square Garden on 28 January 1974.

The day following that fight, Foreman stood to address the nation. He had no trouble following the fastest tongue in town; all he had to do was stand up slowly, giving an adequate impersonation of a genie rising from a bottle. 'I'm no dancer, no singer. I can't tell jokes,' he growled in a smart New York hotel, silhouetted against windows that looked out on Central Park. 'But I'm the best there is at knocking people down.' A Goliath in steel-studded blue denim, Foreman got the range right away. 'I'm going to knock Norton on his ass,' he snarled, attempting to assume the old Liston ogre role.

Foreman had walked out on Ali and Frazier in the fourth round but insisted that he had not meant this to be a dramatic, eye-catching gesture. 'I like fighting. I like being the champion and everything that goes with it. But when I'm not involved, boxing bores me. When it comes to selling fights, I'm no Ali.' He remembered a line from the script. 'I thought success was a destination,' he said, 'now I know it's only another way to travel.'

He was heading towards a bleak experience, but first there would be Norton in Caracas, Venezuela, and a renewal of the belief that no more destructive force had ever emerged in boxing.

I got to Caracas a week before the fight, arriving from Brazil after an attempt to discover whether Pelé would turn out in the World Cup in West Germany. The flight was delayed in Sao Paulo and I had spent two hours in a large, untidy, uninviting lounge, cocooned in transit, the atmosphere depressingly familiar: plastic cups, plastic table tops, plastic anonymity – it could have been any one of a hundred such places dotted around the world.

There were about two dozen people scattered around the room and one of them spoke. 'On your way home?' he asked.

'Caracas,' I replied.

'Business?'

'You could call it that. I'm going to watch a fight. Foreman and Norton.'

'One round,' he said, bluntly. 'Foreman will kill him.'

'You follow the fights?'

'Go to the Garden now and again but mostly on TV. Foreman is something else.'

I nodded, not entirely sure, not yet convinced, but in no mood for prolonged debate and therefore grateful when the flight was called.

Some four hours later, I climbed into a shabby snorting cab, instantly repelled by the stench of petrol, eager for a bath and a bed. Where the hotel once stood, there was a pile of rubble. The driver shrugged. *'Que es esto?'* He shrugged again. Not his problem. Then I remembered where Foreman was staying.

'Lleveme al Hotel Aguila,' I said.

Nothing. No rooms. A hand on my shoulders. 'Hey, howya doin?' It was Dick Sadler and I blurted out my predicament. 'Wait there,' he said, turning to speak with the receptionist. I had a room for one night. One night? 'Once you're in, how they gonna get you out?' Sadler chuckled. 'It's not a problem. Come and get some breakfast.'

Foreman was in the dining-room with Sandy Saddler and Archie Moore and two sparring partners, Terry Hinke, an enormous white heavyweight from Oregon and Eddie 'Boss Man' Jones, a squat light-heavyweight who had the potential to be a champion until he disappeared behind high walls.

None of them spoke very much. 'You seen Norton?' asked Saddler

'Just arrived,' I replied.

Foreman got up and left and eyes followed him across the room. He looked huge and as powerful as I remembered him. 'Great shape,' bubbled Dick Sadler. 'He's ready to go.'

Later that morning, I came across Sandy Saddler, who was leaning against a wall in the shade, a sparse, mild-mannered man afflicted with chronic myopia, but perhaps the most murderous of all featherweight champions – his battles with Willie Pep among the most savage in boxing history. He was as clearly unimpressed by Norton as he was confused by the complexity of intrigue that surrounded the contest. 'I give Norton three rounds,' he rasped. 'A one-track fighter. No moves and there's a dog in there. He'll freeze and run scared.'

There was a persistent rumour that Foreman had already signed to defend against Ali, the contracts lodged in Paris, the most extravagant suggestion, that the fight would take place on a liner in mid-ocean. There was always someone who knew someone who was in on the deal, but it could be assumed that there was one.

Ali's arrival, the next day, fanned the irritation that could be sensed in Norton's camp from the moment that written confirmation of tax clearance failed to arrive.

The challenger trained in secret at an army camp, refusing to co-operate with the promoters until three days before the contest. 'I know how to take Foreman,' he declared confidently, attempting to contradict the widespread opinion that he would not have enough heart to mount a serious challenge 'George is out there with that Sonny Liston stare. Let him take it somewhere else.' He was understandably put out by the rumours. 'Let's say that the winner will fight Ali. That Ken Norton will fight Ali.'

Foreman had his own problems, embroiled in a law suit and threatened by an injunction, his domestic life in turmoil. This appeared to increase Norton's chances substantially, although Pete Hacker, the champion's physician, did not imagine any problems. 'George is in outstanding condition,' he said. 'He's calm and in complete control and has quite remarkable powers of concentration.'

One round. Two. Three? 'Norton goes in three,' repeated Sandy Saddler.

Norton went in the second, experiencing a small death from the moment Foreman climbed into the ring at the Poliedro Stadium to fix him with a withering stare. To go face to face with a man intent on relieving you of your senses is to give irrefutable proof of your courage before a punch is thrown. But Norton's spirit was utterly eroded by the presence of the champion and he was a victim while still on the stool, his eyes those of a terror-stricken hare, his legs trembling. 'I hit a guy and it is like magic. You see him crumbling to the floor. It is a gift from God but only temporary,' Foreman said.

When it was over and Norton had been taken back to his corner, Ali looked across the ring at Foreman as though studying every inch of him. The word was September. The place would be Zaïre. ■

JOE FRAZIER

It has been said for many, many years that you can pick out a Philadelphia fighter from the back of the hall. Nobody has represented this aggressive style more vividly and employed it to greater effect than Joe Frazier, the former slaughterman from South Carolina who engaged Muhammad Ali three times – twice in epic contests for the heavyweight championship.

Frazier's belligerent method, the percussive momentum he developed as an amateur and then brought to the professional ring, did not allow for a backwards step. All his fights were cut to the same ferocious pattern; yet he was no mere slugger relying entirely on raw power and an indomitable will. People compared Frazier with Rocky Marciano but, unlike the only heavyweight champion to retire undefeated, his blows had a cumulative rather than instant effect, so it was more accurate to think of him as a larger version of Henry Armstrong, who held three world titles simultaneously – featherweight, lightweight and welterweight.

Fighting the way he did, taking stiff punches in order to achieve a position from where he could unleash terrible hooks, particularly with the left hand, driving in first to the body and then doubling up to the head, Frazier's career was inevitably short and after losing to Ali in Manila on 1 October 1975, he was an utterly spent force.

The extent of Ali's enduring respect for Frazier is made clear in his autobiography, *The Greatest*:

> For the third time Joe surprised me with his stamina, his relentlessness and the gunpowder in his blows. I opened his lip and closed his eye but he still kept coming, forcing me into the ropes, making me deliver power when I didn't even know if it was still there. It was the same old Joe. The same Joe

Frazier bores in but Ali bears down, using his strength to tie up the challenger . . .

> who dropped me in Madison Square Garden, who shook me round after round again in 1974 before I could take him out. The fight we had in Manila was the next thing to death. I felt like fainting and throwing up and when they wouldn't let Joe come out of his corner for the fifteenth round I was so relieved, so tired and in so much pain that my knees buckled and I stretched out in the middle of the ring. Laying there, drained, I heard the blood pounding in my ears, and in the middle of the pounding, Joe's words came back to me: 'You one bad nigger. We both bad niggers. We don't do no crawlin.'

A handshake bridges the generations. Before defending the Heavyweight Championship against Muhammad Ali at Madison Square Garden in 1971 Joe Frazier poses with Joe Louis, perhaps the greatest of all heavyweights.

In fact Frazier never played his colour up or down. He concentrated on his work and stepped scrupulously aside from racial issues, ignoring the vibrant new militancy with which Ali was so closely identified. As a poor boy helping his father to scratch a living from parched fields, Frazier knew bigotry and discrimination and had a much tougher childhood than Ali, but he was content to pursue the American dream. Thus, at a time of great social strife, he became a symbol of black conservatism.

Frazier was born in Beaufort, South Carolina, on 12 January 1944, the youngest of 13 children and with only a 3 to 1 chance of surviving dietary scourges that had already claimed four of the family. When just 6 years old, he was put to work in the fields, toiling 12 hours a day for a dollar. At 16 he was married and began to feel the restlessness that triggered latent ambition.

'I left the South as soon as I found out about the North,' Frazier told Phil Pepe, his biographer. 'You don't get nowhere standing still. You do that they gonna pass you by. When I decided to leave, I just packed up and left. No huggin' and kissin'. I caught the first thing smokin' North and I left.'

Frazier spent a year in New York and then moved to Philadelphia. And there in a slaughterhouse, stripping sides of beef, at work from 4.30 a.m. until six o'clock at night, he developed the power that was brought to bear on the heavyweight division.

Some outstanding champions were introduced to boxing by enthusiastic police instructors and Frazier's interest took shape when he joined the Twenty-third Police Athletic League gymnasium. He first went there to lose weight but so impressed Duke Dugent, the chief coach, that he called in Yank Durham, a local professional trainer, who recalled: 'One thing impressed me right off. The boy could punch. At first I thought he was just another fat kid who would quit after a few days, but he didn't. He kept coming back. I wasn't involved with him then, I had my own fighters to worry about, but I noticed him. You couldn't help it. He would show up in the gym with his hands cut and tired from working in the slaughterhouse all day. Other guys would stop coming around. Not Joe. He kept coming back and that made you know he was something special.'

Responding quickly to Dugent's tuition, Frazier shortened his punches, fitting them into savage combinations. He learned to double and triple up on the hook, a technique that would become his trade-mark. In 1963 he won the Middle Atlantic Golden Gloves heavyweight championship and, after retaining it the following year, went forward to the Olympic trials. Frazier's record showed only one defeat, a decision to Buster Mathis, and it was Mathis who beat him in the final.

More than 20 years later, a controversial defeat in similar circumstances so disgusted Cus D'Amato that he decided it was time for Mike Tyson, his remarkable young protégé, to turn professional.

When the judges declared Mathis the winner in 1964 and therefore

String puller – string player. Joe Frazier was guided to Heavyweight Championship by Yank Durham, their partnership formed on mean streets in Philadelphia.

their Olympic heavyweight choice, Frazier became so depressed that he threatened to give up boxing. Instead, he agreed to join the Olympic squad as a sparring partner and took full advantage of astonishing good fortune.

In an exhibition bout Mathis broke a finger on Frazier's head and withdrew from the team. As a result, Frazier went to Tokyo and, despite a broken left thumb that severely reduced his effectiveness in the final against Hans Huber of West Germany, he became the first American to win an Olympic heavyweight championship.

The injury delayed Frazier's professional début until 16 August 1965 when, trained by Yank Durham, he was paid $500 to fight at the Philadelphia Convention Hall. It was immediately clear that Frazier might struggle to emulate Muhammad Ali and Floyd Patterson, who went on to win the world heavyweight championship as former Olympic gold medallists. He was still crude and, in the opinion of many good judges, too short in the leg and arm. Enormous thighs provided a power base but made lateral movement difficult and tiring so that if Frazier attempted to out-jab opponents, he was bound to be picked off. Realizing this, Durham concentrated on natural strength and determination and devised a style that required Frazier to pound forward, absorbing punishment as he built up a destructive tempo.

Although confident that his man could take a punch, Durham nevertheless shuddered when Frazier, in his second professional contest, was sent down by Mike Bruce. 'Until the first time you can never be sure,' Durham recalled. Frazier regained the upright position and battered out Bruce in the third round.

It was time to look for sponsors and Frazier signed with Cloverlay Incorporated, a consortium of Philadelphia business men formed to promote his career. To begin with, Frazier received $100 a week plus 50 per cent of his purses, half in cash the rest to be invested. The investors retained 35 per cent, out of which they met all expenses. The remaining 15 per cent went to Durham, who was given a free hand as manager and trainer.

The early part of Frazier's professional career took familiar shape. Carefully matched in the manner of all promising young fighters, he recorded 11 straight victories, all by knock-out, and was thought to be a future heavyweight contender.

Frazier's first serious test came against Oscar Bonavena on 21 Septemer 1966 – a fortnight after Ali defeated Karl Mildenberger to retain the undisputed championship. Two men whose careers are inextricably linked were coming together, but boxing is a mysterious business and had Frazier not withstood the impact of a punch fired into his jaw at Madison Square Garden, they might never have met in the ring.

There was little to suggest that Bonavena would be a serious threat to Frazier. A burly but limited brawler from Argentina, he was more durable than dangerous, with no reputation as a puncher; but in the second, blood already streaming from a cut over the left eye, he threw a desperate right that scrambled Frazier's senses.

Fighters cannot be taught how to react in such bleak circumstances, as Jimmy Tibbs explained before Frank Bruno challenged Mike Tyson for the championship in February 1989. Bruno has no survival instinct. When struck hard, he drops his hands and lurches backwards, an open target for further punishment. Tibbs, a former professional middleweight who had trained the British heavyweight, said: 'To get through the crisis you rely on an inner sense. The first time it happened I found myself hanging on, grabbing, holding, staying in close, instinct takes over.'

Frazier struggled to his feet and survived the round. By the fourth, head clear again, he began to dominate the contest and won a unanimous decision.

Two months later, Frazier defeated Eddie Machen in Los Angeles and six victories in 1967 established him as a considerable force in the division. In April of that year Ali defied the draft-board – an assertion of independence that led to three years' exile from the ring.

In view of their awesome tussles, it is interesting to reflect on how Frazier might have fared when Ali was at his peak. It is generally agreed that this was reached in November 1966 when he took Cleveland Williams apart in Houston, Texas, displaying the full range of his thrilling virtuosity. To have fought Ali at that time would surely have been disastrous for Frazier, but it can be supposed that the match would have been made if only to satisfy widespread disapproval of the champion's refusal to be conscripted.

The World Boxing Association and then the New York Boxing Commission moved with pathetic haste to strip Ali of his titles and set up a series of eliminators, involving Floyd Patterson, Jimmy Ellis, Thad Spencer, Bonavena, Ernie Terrell, Mildenberger, Jerry Quarry and Frazier.

Frazier wanted no part of it and on 4 March 1968 took a share of the championship, stopping Buster Mathis at Madison Square Garden in a contest approved by the states of New York, Illinois, Pennsylvania, Maine, Texas and Massachusetts.

Jimmy Ellis, a pumped-up middleweight shrewdly managed by Angelo Dundee, finally emerged as the WBA champion, but it was two

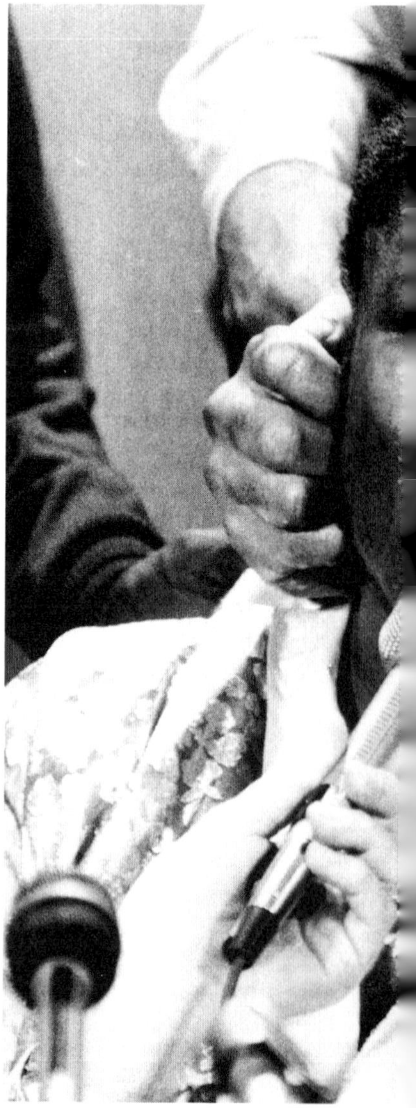

After defeating Ali at Madison Square Garden New York in March 1971, Joe Frazier was in hospital for a week. Yank Durham applies an ice pack to his face at the post fight press conference.

The Thrilla in Manila. Muhammad Ali, his face bearing the marks of Joe Frazier's blows, reaches out again for his greatest adversary . . .

years before he fought Frazier to unify the title. Ellis lasted only five rounds.

On 26 October 1970, Ali returned to the ring in Atlanta, Georgia, and knocked out Jerry Quarry in the third round. On 7 December he stopped Bonavena. Frazier versus Ali was drawing closer. They came together at Madison Square Garden on 8 March 1971, sharing $5 million, the first of the televized Super Fights attracting a world-wide audience of 300 million in 46 countries. There were no complaints. A marvellous contest went the distance and any doubts that Frazier was ahead dissolved in the fifteenth round when Ali went down from a vicious left hook.

Frazier had at last established himself as the undisputed champion, but a new force had emerged. On 22 January 1973, Frazier defended the title against George Foreman in Kingston, Jamaica, and was knocked out in the second round, utterly devastated by the challenger's immense power. In all, Frazier went down six times before the referee, Arthur Mercante, stopped the fight.

This upset led to dramatic happenings. After narrowly outpointing Frazier in New York on 28 January 1974, Ali completed the resurrection when he knocked out Foreman in Zaïre to regain the championship. A year later, in the Philippines, Frazier and Ali met again. At the end of the fourteenth round, Eddie Futch, trainer since Yank Durham's death, cut the gloves from Frazier's hands.

'I kept thinking what a wonderful father Joe is,' he said, 'I thought about his kids and how much he loves them. I didn't want him to end up a cabbage.'

Although Frazier fought twice more – a five-round loss to Foreman and a draw with Floyd 'Jumbo' Cummings – a noble warrior's career ended that morning in Manila. ■

LARRY HOLMES

In an era other than that dominated by the most remarkable heavyweight in history, Larry Holmes would have gained the status he craved throughout his career.

Holmes lived in the shadow of a legend, Muhammed Ali, and was therefore denied the credit he deserved for almost equalling Rocky Marciano's record of 49 straight victories – falling one short when Michael Spinks won the International Boxing Federation championship on a close decision in Las Vegas in 1987.

On 2 October 1980, Holmes defended his championship against an ageing Ali who had once employed him as a sparring partner.

* * * * *

The contest was only a month away, so I interrupted a holiday in California and flew east, taking the red-eye overnight from San Diego to New York, then driving to where Holmes could be found at work in his home town, Easton, Pennsylvania. It was only a hour or so by road from there to Ali's training camp at Deer Lake and the plan was to see him the next day.

On the way across I thought a lot about Holmes. He was wealthy by then, many times a millionaire, but it had not taken long to pay him out the very first time. Just one hundred dollars in tens and fives and a few grubby singles: you do not get rich boxing down the bill in Scranton, Pennsylvania.

Holmes had beaten a long-forgotten Rodell Dupree on 21 March 1973, and it was time to collect. Ernie Butler, who managed him in those days, took some off the top and handed over the rest. It came to $63 and Butler saw disappointment leap into the young heavyweight's narrow eyes.

Sixty-three dollars.

Holmes closed a large fist around the thin fold of green notes and thought about it all. Those achingly cold dawns on the road; the punches he had to take and old guys in the gym with beat-up faces who preached that sex would take away his strength.

Sixty-three dollars.

Breaking the silence that had settled upon a sparse dressing-room, Butler attempted to encourage his young fighter. 'Come on,' he enthused. 'It's a start. Give me ten dollars and I'll open a bank account for you in the morning.'

Holmes smiled. A bank account? Hell, he knew dudes who believed that banks were only for robbing.

Since that night, Holmes had earned millions, but he lived a long time in long shadows. He left school at 13 and on the meanest of Easton's streets he encountered bigotry and racial strife. People came to respect an impressive left jab but they were not so sure about his heart. For a long time, he also fought

Larry Holmes, 'The Easton Assassin', the most underrated of modern heavyweight champions.

LARRY HOLMES

The long and lonely road leads to Las Vegas for Larry Holmes as he prepares to fight Muhammad Ali for the Heavyweight Championship.

in the shadows, a hired hand, sparring with Ali and Joe Frazier, determined to be somebody.

In Manila on 1 October 1975, he stopped Rodney Bobick in six rounds; but it was the day Ali and Frazier fought themselves to a standstill, so nobody cared. Then, in 1978, Holmes outpointed Ken Norton to win the World Boxing Council heavyweight title and he was on his way; now he was going in with Ali.

A violent image came hurtling out of memory: Las Vegas, September 1979; a caveman's blow – a primitive, clubbing right that suddenly separated Holmes from his senses, the paralysis instant. Holmes went down, his huge frame a mess of disconnected tissue and the ring shuddered like a stricken ship. From that moment, when the shaven-headed veteran Earnie Shavers blasted into him midway through the seventh round, Holmes was given an opportunity to prove that he had genuine fighting heart and a strong chin.

The crowd gasped, then roared and in Shavers' corner there was fresh hope and leaping pandemonium. Holmes could not have heard any of it; for him there was only blackness and near oblivion. He reached one knee, then his feet, but the nightmare was not over; his eyes vacant, unsteady on jellied legs that moved in opposite directions.

'Go get him, Earnie,' screamed the challenger's corner men, knowing that riches were only another raw right hand away.

Shavers, both eyes cut and bleeding but strength renewed, came on like a crazed mugger and it probably cost him the championship. Holmes wobbled, hanging on, reaching out of the bleakness for the man who had so nearly destroyed him, the survival instinct still strong. Then the bell and a frustrated Shavers lumbered back to his corner, the faint smile playing on his battered face clearly one of resignation.

It would be a while before the mist cleared from Holmes's brain, but in the eighth he began to box again and for Shavers there was now only the prospect of a painful experience. The jab began to jump back into his battered face, sometimes sliding up into the worsening lacerations. If it was not the jab, it was a hook: a heavy, hurtful right, employed by Holmes so that he was invariably moving away from, rather than into, the line of retaliatory fire.

Shavers, hands down, began to lurch from one crisis to another and whenever Holmes would allow it, he gulped in air. He was 35 but looked ten years older.

There was not much time left for the challenger. He smiled his smile and Holmes, as though fearful of inflicting permanent damage, pleaded for the fight to be stopped. Shavers rejected the chance to quit but offered no protest when the referee's restraining arms brought an end to the contest after two minutes of the eleventh round.

'Yes, I asked the referee to stop it,' Holmes confirmed. 'I said, "Look, I'm killing this guy. Is that what you want me to do?" I was telling Earnie to quit. He was a good contender. He'd given everything, so I said, "Why don't you quit man? Why do you want to take all this pain?" But he just keeps smiling at me, telling me that quitting isn't his way.'

The past dissolved and I turned off the freeway and followed the signs to Easton, making for the hotel where I had arranged to meet my friend Bob Waters of *Newsday*, who had travelled down from his home on Long Island. Bob was at the bar, gazing reflectively at what was left in his glass. From experience I knew that it had begun as a Beefeater Martini, seven parts gin to one part vermouth and, applying the Archimedes principle, no fruit. 'He's working out at two,' Bob said.

We arrived in time to hear Holmes messing up a poem. 'Where's my poem?' he bellowed, feeding a hand into the hip pocket of smart tan slacks. 'It's a good poem, better than Ali's poems.'

It was not a good poem.

'On October second this is the thing. Ali meets Holmes in the middle of the ring; Ali swings his left then his right, but Holmes knocks him outta sight . . .' He fumbled for the next elusive line and then spat out his frustration. 'Dammit, I forgot again, but you can all fill it in yourselves.'

'Hey, Larry, leave the poems to Muhammed,' said a bystander, cheekily.

Holmes rounded on him. 'I'm leaving that guy with nothin',' he declared. 'No name. Nothin'. This is gonna be Ali's Last Hurrah.' The words spoke of resentment. Holmes was the champion but he sensed that Ali remained the number one man. Holmes was a name; Ali, inescapably, a legend, a happening, an era. Holmes could not rid himself of that and he wanted to take a stake to Ali, plunge it through his heart so that the legend would be no more. 'I know you all have sentiment for Ali,' he added, 'but don't make no mistake. Don't make no foolish bets. The fight can't go ten rounds. He'll tire out and I'll take him out. I know him better than he knows himself. Ali is thirty-eight and he's fat. He can take off the weight but he can't take off the years and he's been hit too many times. Those hurts come back on a fighter. Hell, he don't psyche me out. How's he gonna do that? I was his sparring partner on and off for four years. I had orders to hit him on the arms and shoulders, not to hit him in the head.'

Did Holmes expect Ali to go for him toe-to-toe, trying for an early knock-out?

'I hope that's the way he wants to play it,' Holmes growled, going an octave lower for emphasis. 'I ain't gonna run and he knows it.'

All eyes on Ali, three times the Heavyweight Champion, as he prepares to fight Larry Holmes . . .

Holmes looked across to where his baby daughter was being dangled over a bannister. 'Get her off there,' he shouted angrily, 'get her away from there.' The champion shook his head. 'God I wish I could get that mad at Ali,' he said. 'Ali came to Easton when I was just a kid and I hitched a ride on his bus. Man I was up there in the clouds.'

The next morning, we pulled out of a motel and made for Deer Lake, finally climbing the hill that led to Ali's training camp.

Mirror, mirror on the wall, who is greatest of them all? The mirror was Ali's friend. It turned back the clock; it reflected his youth. It told him he was still the prettiest, the greatest. The mirror could not reflect the inner Ali, but it nourished his pride.

'Look at me,' he proclaimed, glancing sideways at the framed glass, devastatingly trim in tailored slacks and a form-fitting black shirt. 'Look at me. Isn't that sumthin'? I'm thirty-eight but I look twenty-nine. I was up to two thirty-five pounds, now I am down to two twenty-two. No sugar, no sodas, no milk – only water. I'm as thin as I was when I fought Henry Cooper. My wife and my mother are shocked by the change in me. Larry Holmes is shocked, the universe is shocked.'

Ali was approaching his sixtieth professional contest and had submitted himself to an extensive medical at the Mayo Clinic in Minnesota.

ALI
EVERLAST
EVERLAST

EVERLAST

Nothing much left. Ali comes out for the tenth round against Holmes. Drew 'Bundini' Brown and Walter Youngblood urge him on but Angelo Dundee looks apprehensive.

The well runs dry. Ali slumps disconsolately in his corner at the end of the fourteenth round against Larry Holmes in Las Vegas. Holmes, once his sparring partner, still the Heavyweight Champion. Ali would fight once more, his career coming to an end in Nassau, in the Bahamas, when outpointed by Trevor Berbick in November 1981.

'They cleared me,' he said, 'so why should people think I am in danger? You think I'm going to get hurt? When did I ever get hurt?' A breeze came off Ali's fingers as he faked a jab at Bob Waters's head. A following right created more turbulence. 'Holmes can jab but sometimes he don't go all the way. When that happens, POW, I'll get him with a straight right. If he throws combinations, I'll just cover up and tire him out. He'll look for me to dance, run, rope-a-dope, but I'll be going for him.'

Ali had written a new villain into an old script.

Bob Waters had been around Ali from the beginning and he understood fighters. 'The guy is finished. There isn't anything left,' he said suddenly on the way back to New York.

There was not, but a month later it seemed that only a severe beating would persuade Ali that he was an utterly spent force. Within six hours of being stopped for the first time, he declared his intention to fight again. Deaf to the legitimate concern being expressed by his friends, he could not accept that the old man with a scythe has yet to drop a decision.

In a ring raised over the car-park at Caesar's Palace, the atmosphere oddly reminiscent of a bygone era in boxing, Ali was pitiful and a less compassionate opponent would have battered him senseless into oblivion. As he was led away, stumbling, dull-eyed with exhaustion beneath a canopy of exploding fireworks, Ali looked old – old like they all do when the well runs dry.

They laid Ali down and Holmes, fearful of what he might have done, came to sit with him.

'Hey, you're real bad,' Ali mumbled painfully, twisting his head from the pillows.

'Look at the teacher I had,' replied Holmes. 'But tell me you aren't gonna fight again.'

Ali eased his face back into the linen, muffling his voice to emphasize the mischief. 'I'm coming back for Holmes,' he moaned. 'Holmes, Holmes . . .'

Holmes smiled and left.

The world was not greeted the next day with news of Ali's retirement, but with a blatant refusal to accept reality. 'I want Mike Weaver,' he said when appearing on breakfast television, speaking from the centre of the ring.

Weaver held the World Boxing Association version of the championship and was due to defend it against Gerrie Coetzee in South Africa.

There was a hurried consultation in Ali's suite and he was advised to back off from the statement. He wandered through the rooms, pausing to study his reflection. 'Hmm, I look OK, I feel OK,' he said before addressing his lawyer, Michael Phenner: 'We get the money?'

'Take it easy with that Weaver stuff,' advised Phenner.

Ali fingered the soreness on his face and

Ol' Blue Eyes meets the Great White Hope. Gerry Cooney in training to challenge Larry Holmes for the Heavyweight Championship.

spoke about being dehydrated in the fight, of feeling sticky and unable to perspire. 'All of us have been losing in some way,' he said. 'There is a time for love. There is a time for hate. A time for success. A time for failure.'

In his mind, Ali was still the champion and Larry Holmes knew it. ■

ROBERTO DURAN

When this picture was taken in Las Vegas in June 1986, Roberto Duran apeared to be clinging to the remnants of his career, no longer a champion, fighting on the undercard, surplus flesh creased above the waistband of his shorts. Amazingly he would win two championships, defeating Iran Barkley for the IBF Middleweight title when 37 years old.

Late on 25 November 1980 a small group of men, a dozen, maybe less, waited in the corridor outside a suite on the fourteenth floor of an hotel in New Orleans; some lounged against the walls, one or two sprawled untidily on the floor, their frustration evident in weary postures and murmured complaints. When the door of the suite opened to admit a visitor, those on the floor got up quickly and all the men pressed forward. For a moment they could see inside the room and one of them spoke up. 'Is he going to talk to us?' he asked irritably. There was no response; the door closed and the men dispersed, shaking their heads, grumbling as they made towards the lifts. 'That's a quitter for you,' one said.

Inside the room Roberto Duran rose from a chair and crossed to where he could look down on the lights of the city. He bit fiercely into an orange, spat out the peel and sucked hard on the juice. His companions – two of them bearing the marks of age and conflict on their gnarled faces – remained discreetly silent.

A few hours earlier, Duran had gone to his corner to defend the world welterweight championship against Sugar Ray Leonard, established beyond all legitimate doubt as the most savagely effective fighter at work in the game. There were many stories about Duran. It was said that, when a boy of only 12 years, he had struck down grown men with his bare fists in Chorrillo, a grim, wind-raked barrio that lies on the east side of the mouth of the Panama Canal, across from Fort Amador. It was also said that he used to make daily raids on the mango plantations, swimming two miles across the Canal, a knife held between his teeth. One of eight children, Duran sold the mangoes to help his abandoned mother raise her family. He busked in the streets, singing and dancing for tips and when fully grown knocked a horse senseless with a single blow.

The low blow that ended Buchanan's resistance when losing the championship to Roberto Duran.

In the professional ring Duran could be instantly identified as a violently malevolent spirit – more likely to snarl and spit than observe traditional formalities – and his savage style evoked awe. He was known as *Manos de Piedra* (Hands of Stone).

Duran's father, an itinerant American soldier from Arizona, part-Indian, part-Mexican, deserted his mother before he was born on 16 June 1951. At 13 Duran was expelled from school for punching an older assailant down a flight of steps. A year later, he turned to boxing after following his brother Domingo to a gymnasium supervised by Nestor Quinones. At just 16, he was already a feared professional.

Carlos Eleta, a millionaire racehorse owner and a former tennis champion of Panama with substantial influence in Latin American sport, had not forgotten the youngster he caught stealing coconuts and bought his contract in 1971 from Alfredo Vasquez, a Panamanian jockey.

Duran, squat and swarthy, with powerful shoulders and hair black as a raven's wings, would not have looked out of place in an Apache raid. He fought crudely, a natural brawler, undertaking every contest as a brutal test of strength and will. In order to improve him, Eleta lured Ray Arcel out of retirement. Arcel, then 72, was one of the most respected trainers in American boxing and had helped mould 16 world champions, including Barney Ross, Tony Zale, Ezzard Charles and the Englishman, Jack 'Kid' Berg. At Arcel's suggestion, Eleta also hired Freddie Brown, another legendary veteran.

The primitive urge to batter opponents into submission was such a powerful element in Duran's nature that it was a while before the old men were able to refine his raw talent. Patiently, they taught him to cut off escape routes and how a hurtful left could be employed as a triggering

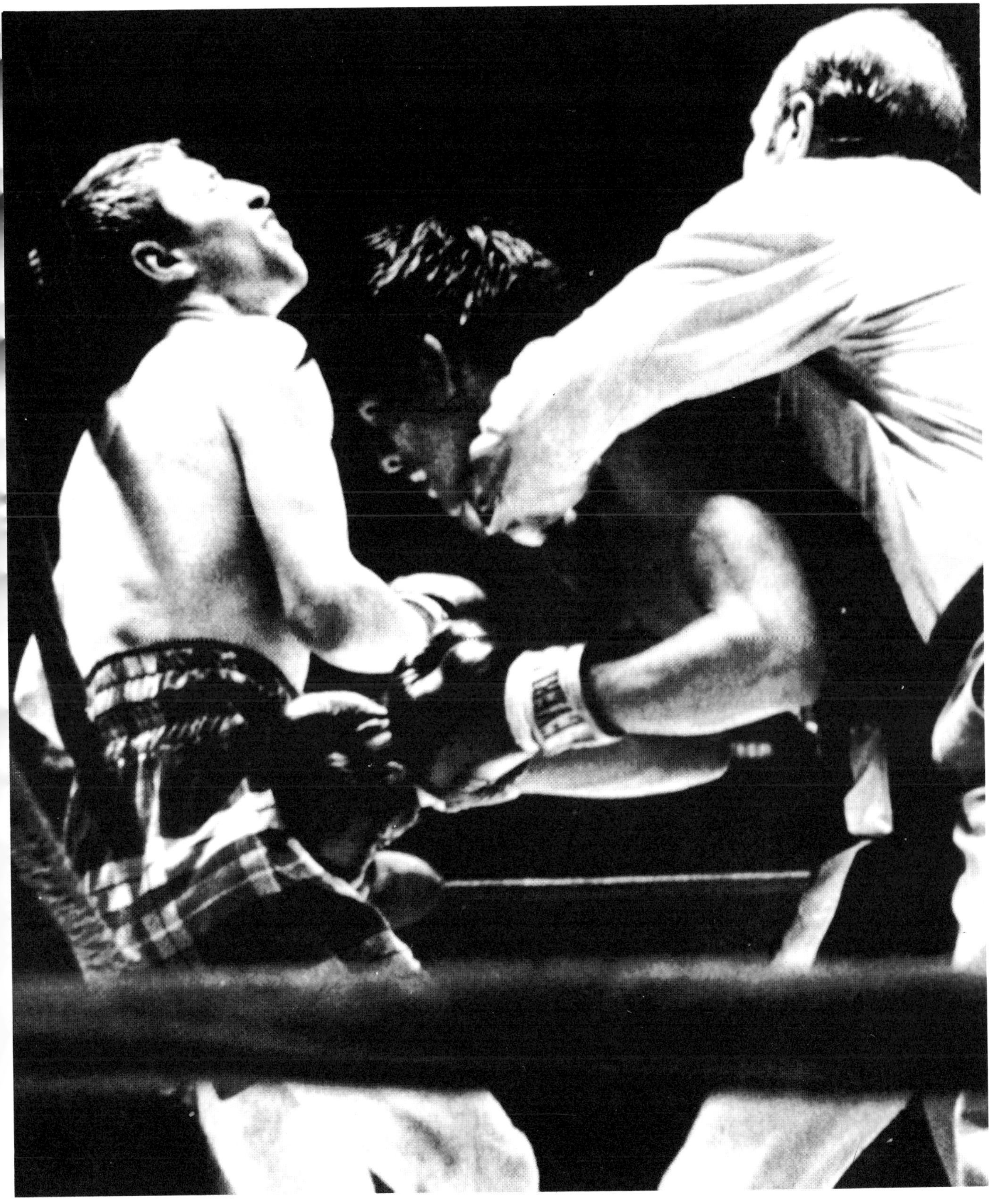

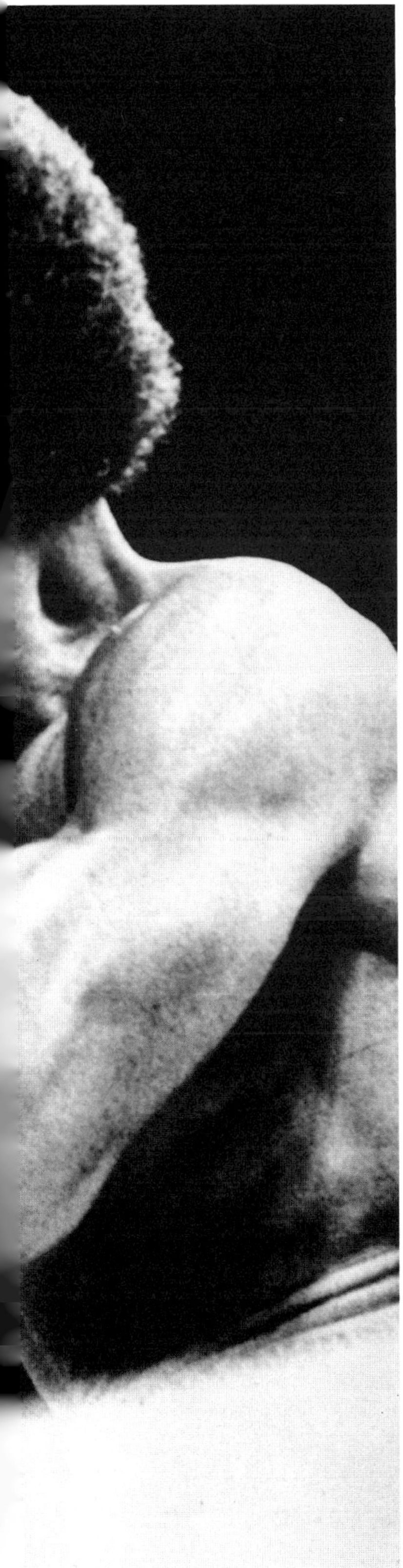

Before the surrender. Roberto Duran and Sugar Ray Leonard at close quarters in their second fight for the Welterweight Championship on 25 November 1980. Bemused by the tactics and debilitated by a weight problem, Duran quit, in the eighth round, claiming he had severe cramp.

mechanism for a naturally chilling right; they showed him how to slip punches by bobbing his head when launching ferocious assaults.

By the time Duran fought Ken Buchanan for the lightweight championship at Madison Square Garden, New York, on 20 January 1972, he was unbeaten and only four of 28 opponents had remained upright until the final bell. Buchanan, a fiercely independent Scot who ranks as one of the most accomplished boxers to represent Britain since the Second World War, took the title from Ismael Laguna in San Juan, Puerto Rico, on 20 September 1970. He had defended it twice, most thrillingly in a return against Laguna. He had lost just one of 44 contests – a controversial decision in Madrid. Despite growing respect for Duran's relentlessly aggressive method, he was made an 8 to 5 on favourite.

Some years later, Duran expressed admiration for Buchanan; but that night in New York he lived up fully to a vivid impression conveyed by Sam Toperoff in his book *Sugar Ray Leonard and other Noble Warriors*:

> Duran was not a one-punch knockout artist; rather, he beat on and came forward incessantly, finally putting the other fighter away after some invisible tolerance and survival threshold had been crossed. A typical Duran victory usually evoked the same key words from the boxing writers, words like 'savage', 'disdainful', 'brutal', 'pitiless'. There were no other fighters quite like him in the 1970s. He was a throwback in more ways than one, a mysterious, dark figure from some tropical and mythic past.

For all his ringcraft and experience, Buchanan could not interrupt Duran's percussive rhythm and was continually forced back against the ropes. When the bell sounded to end the thirteenth round, both men

Beyond belief, Roberto Duran, '*no mas*-no more,' indicates that he has taken enough from Sugar Ray Leonard in their welterweight title fight in New Orleans on 25 November 1980.

continued punching and Duran, ever eager to flaunt the rules, drove a wicked blow into Buchanan's groin. After being hauled back to his corner in pain, the Scot indicated he was prepared to continue, but the referee stopped the contest. Duran, at 21, was the new champion.

On his return to Panama, a crowd of more than 5,000 greeted him at the airport. Thousands more lined the streets as he made for Chorrillo, waving from an open car. In Duran's world, escaping from the gutter was an accomplishment. But the malignant urchin had achieved more: his rage, legitimized in the cruellest of sports, had made him into a national hero.

Duran went on to dominate the lightweight division, being successful in 14 defences – the only blemish on his record: a defeat against Estaban DeJesus in a non-title match when recovering from an illness. He met DeJesus twice after that and battered him senseless both times.

In February 1978, Duran relinquished the 9 st 9 lb championship. By then he had a spacious home in Nuevo Reparto El Carmen, one of the most select communities in Panama, and among the rewards for being a champion was exemption from taxes. He bought his mother a house and invested in property.

As a lightweight, Duran won all but one of 63 contests, including 51 knock-outs. As a welterweight, he proved to be less destructive; the result not of diminished power but of larger men being better able to withstand the impact of his punches. For example, Bob Foster did some terrible damage as a light-heavyweight, but he was knocked out in the second round when challenging Joe Frazier for the heavyweight championship.

Duran dismissed the theory but was nevertheless taken the full distance of ten rounds in his first three fights at 10 st 7 lb. The second fight was against Carlos Palomino, a former champion. Palomino went down in the opening session, but recovered to give Duran a hard fight. 'As a lightweight it seemed he was tremendous puncher,' Palomino said afterwards. 'But I didn't find him to be that kind of puncher as a welterweight. A good puncher, a strong puncher but not a devastating puncher.'

Hagler shakes Duran with a left hook when defending the middleweight Championship in Las Vegas.

It was inevitable that Duran would be matched with Sugar Ray Leonard for the championship and they came together in Montreal on 20 June 1980. Leonard, the colourful master craftsman, an Olympic gold medallist, was fully installed as an American hero, the antithesis of a man some called El Animal.

Leonard, astonishingly, chose to fight on Duran's terms as if determined to prove he had as much heart for the raw extremities of boxing. After 15 rounds, the exchanges unrelentingly bitter, Duran was declared the new champion.

Five months later, they fought again in New Orleans. In the meantime Duran had grown so fat he was required to train off 20 pounds. He appeared dull, less belligerent. Leonard taunted Duran, frustrating him with extravagant manoeuvres that were an insult to machismo. Suddenly, in the eighth round, Duran dropped his hands and said, '*No peleo mas*.' (I fight no more.) He had surrendered and his career was in disarray. The shame of it accompanied Duran back to Panama. There were no crowds at the airport and he discovered insults scrawled on the walls of his home.

Anybody who climbs into the ring is offering irrefutable proof of his courage and yet, in a cruel business, it is considered unforgivable to give up under punishment. Duran's behaviour has never been adequately explained, but he continued to fight and restored some of his reputation

on 16 June 1983 when taking the World Boxing Association light-middleweight title from Davey Moore, becoming only the seventh in history to win world titles at three weights.

The old warrior snarls his disrespect for Robbie Sims.

In November of the same year Duran was outpointed by Marvelous Marvin Hagler when challenging for the middleweight championship in Las Vegas; but, in a ring erected behind Caesar's Palace, he made Hagler nervous and was seen again to be one of the most evil great fighters of all time.

When Thomas Hearns, defending the WBC super-welterweight title in June 1984, knocked him out before the second round was completed, Duran did not appear to have much left. As this applied equally to a squandered fortune, he was forced to accept the embarrassment of boxing down the bill.

Then, on 24 February 1989, at the Convention Hall in Atlantic City, New Jersey, he fought Iran Barkley for the WBC middleweight championship. Duran was 37 and had been boxing professionally for almost 22 years, so the odds favoured Barkley, a strong puncher who had pulverized Hearns to win the championship.

It turned out to be one of the most thrilling contests for years, one that fully replenished the Duran legend. 'Iran Barkley is full of himself because he beat Hearns and Hearns beat me,' Duran had said, 'But I wasn't in shape for that fight. I was sick. This time I promise the Panamanian people I will be 100 per cent fit. I have built up my strength.'

Going in at 11 st 2½ lb, calling on all he has ever learned in the ring, Duran continually brought the crowd to its feet and a great roar of excitement went up when he floored Barkley with a classic combination in the eleventh round – a right, followed by a stunning left hook, then

That's how it used to be – Duran staggers Robbie Sims with a characteristically vicious left hook.

two more rights to the head. The champion, six inches taller and nine years the younger man, was so stunned after taking a mandatory eight count that he had trouble finding his corner at the end of the round. Barkley recovered in time to stage an impressive rally in the final session and some felt he had done enough to retain his title.

When they broke off at the final bell, Duran stood sideways on, feet planted, snarling belligerently before returning to his corner. Then, completely out of character, burrowing through the crowd that had gathered in the ring, he crossed to Barkley's corner and embraced him.

In a split decision, two of the three judges voted for Duran and he was installed once again as a great legend of the game. The shame of New Orleans had been completely erased and, predictably, he wanted Leonard again. ■

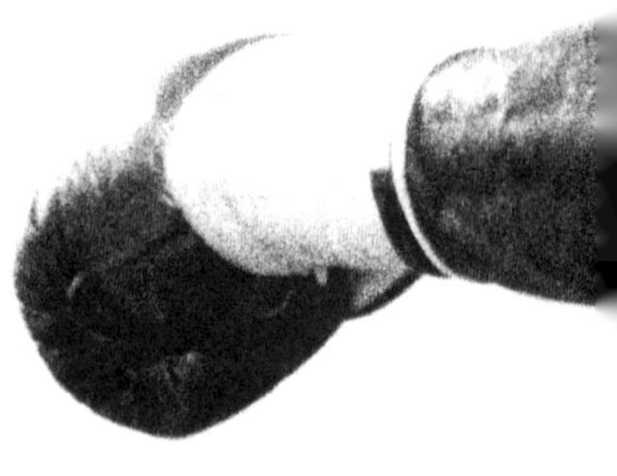

KEN BUCHANAN

The suggestion is bound to provoke a few arguments in Belfast, Liverpool, London and Merthyr Tydfil, but it is difficult to think of anyone who has represented British Boxing more thrillingly since the Second World War than Ken Buchanan, the Edinburgh carpenter who became lightweight champion of the world.

When Buchanan went to his corner in San Juan, Puerto Rico, on 26 September 1970, the temperature hovering at 100 degrees, no Briton had won a world championship abroad for 55 years and he was given little chance against Ismael Laguna, the champion from Panama.

Despite badly cut eyes and the intimidating clamour of a predominantly Hispanic audience, Buchanan gained a split decision over 15 rounds and consolidated his status four months later by outpointing Ruben Navarro in Los Angeles.

Between times, Buchanan fought Donato Paduano, a Canadian welterweight, at Madison Square Garden, and it was this contest that excited comparisons with even the great Sugar Ray Robinson.

A successful defence against Laguna further established Buchanan's reputation in New York, where he was always better received than in his native land, even after losing the championship to Roberto Duran who was perhaps the most complete fighter ever to appear in the 9 st 6 lb division.

Difficult, moody, soured by teenage experiences, but unquestionably a notable talent, Buchanan tried unsuccessfully to regain the title from Ishimatsu Suzuki, losing a 15-round decision in Tokyo on 27 February 1975. He retired five months later after defeating Giancarlo Usai to retain his European Championship.

It should have been enough, but in 1980 Buchanan resumed his career in the all-too-familiar role of a hard-up fighter, left only with the remnants of the talent that had thrilled the Garden.

On 24 November 1980 he was paid barely £1,500 to box Lance Williams on the undercard at Wembley Arena, and was adjudged to have lost narrowly after eight punishing rounds.

* * * * *

Ken Buchanan peered into the mirror set on a wall of his cramped quarters, carefully peeling back bruised lips so that he could examine the cuts hidden inside. The soreness made him wince, and he saw a face that was no longer his own. Somebody asked why he was there.

'Money,' Buchanan replied bluntly.

He sank tender fingers into swollen cheeks, studying the distortive effect of punches that would not have touched him in the now long ago. The mirror was telling Buchanan the truth; it was telling him to quit.

'Just one more,' he mumbled, turning away from the reflection, the words coming thick, because his nose would not be working properly for a while.

Just one more. Just one more.

Since returning to the ring two years earlier,

Few British fighters have made a greater impact than Ken Buchanan, the Edinburgh carpenter who became Lightweight Champion of the World, but he lost the title when exposed to the ferocious power generated by Roberto Duran, the primitive from Panama.

Buchanan, by then 37 years old, had lost four of eight contests. The former lightweight champion had become, painfully, just another fighter in another ring.

He was booked to fight in Nigeria, the following month, hoping that a decent purse would help him buy into a public house.

Just one more. Just one more.

There was a tragic Hollywood touch to Buchanan's plight, echoes of *The Champion*, *Golden Boy* and *Body and Soul*. The old pro clutching at one last pay-day.

Blood was still seeping from Buchanan's swollen nose and where once there had been the agitation of clamour and acclaim, there was now only embarrassment. Some of us thought about other nights in other places. We remembered the wall-to-wall crush, the dazzle of television lights, thrusting notebooks and the frenzied squeak of fibre-tipped pens. It was Kenny this and Kenny that and who would you like to fight next?

Now it was just one more. Just one more time.

We remembered how it was for Buchanan against Duran in the Garden: the savage exchanges and how much respect the murderous Panamanian had for him.

And we remembered him taking to the dance floor with Princess Anne in a smart London hotel: a bright-eyed, sharp-faced Sportsman of the Year.

Roberto Duran snarls behind a powerful right that sends Ken Buchanan back against the ropes.

Buchanan retained the body of a young man; the shoulders well shaped, his abdomen a washboard of rippling muscle, but the face in that dressing-room was that of a pensioner.

'Look at him,' said Paddy Byrne, an astute Irish matchmaker and promoter who had negotiated all Buchanan's come-back contests. 'He's kept himself in tremendous shape but the strength is no longer there and he gets caught because the reflexes dull with time. There's nothing to keep young fellas like Williams away. There was a time when he would have demolished a boy like that but not any more. I want him to turn it in and he will after the fight in Nigeria. He's promised.

'Kenny should make enough to get himself into a business and if he wants to manage a couple of fighters, I'll get them work. It's so sad that he has to go on fighting like this.'

Buchanan had assured the British Boxing Board of Control that his come-back was drawing to a close.

'Kenny has been an enormous credit to the game and we've allowed him to continue boxing because he hasn't been taking any beatings,' said Ray Clarke, then the secretary. 'But I think his time is up.'

There had been illuminating flashes of what Buchanan was when he took the championship from Laguna, particularly when a left hook so rattled Williams that he went down, his temporary plight suggesting that it might be an easy night for the Scot. But Williams recovered and, although his own work was never immediately decisive, the cumulative effect of a younger man's blows became evident.

At the back of the hall, Eddie Thomas turned away, no longer wanting to look. Before their relationship ended in rancorous dispute, Thomas, the most notable figure in modern Welsh boxing, had managed Buchanan and had taken him to the title.

Thomas had mapped out a similar route for Colin Jones, the Welsh welterweight from Gorseinen who fought three times for the world championship. Buchanan was yesterday's man. Jones was about tomorrow, but Thomas had sentiment to spare. 'Damn it man, I couldn't watch Kenny out there,' he said. 'I kept turning away, wanting to run from it. Fighters should be protected from themselves. The trouble is that they don't thank you for telling them to quit. I've had my share of that. But if it was up to me, I wouldn't let Kenny box again.'

Buchanan padded wearily away to the showers and let the soothing warmth play over his wounds.

Just one more. Just one more time. ■

Buchanan sets up Carlos Hernandez for an eight-round knockout in London.

MARVIN HAGLER

There was something about the way Marvelous Marvin Hagler went about his work that ought to have made believers of us all; not just the energy and the drive, but simple things like carrying his own bag and smearing grease on his face: those things said a lot about one of the great middleweight champions. They spoke of deprivation and prejudice and the terror he experienced as a boy when sheltering from riots that claimed 26 lives in Newark, New Jersey. They spoke also about frustration and occasional despair.

'What else have you got?' Marvin Hagler turns away from Sugar Ray Leonard and makes for his corner at the end of the fifth round of their Middleweight contest in Las Vegas on 6 April 1987.

Hagler was 28 when he took the undisputed 11 st 6 lb title from Alan Minter at Wembley Arena in London on 27 September 1980 and by then had suffered plenty for his independence. Side-tracked by promoters, dodged by champions, embittered by a controversial draw against Vito Antuofermo, he came to prominence the hard way.

It seemed as though Hagler always had something to prove. 'It was difficult,' he said, 'because I didn't want to be like Jersey Joe Walcott, getting older but not getting the praise. I remember asking myself what I had to do to impress. Did I have to kill somebody in order to let the world know I was alive? People may have thought they were cutting out my heart, but they were only making me meaner.'

A devastatingly powerful and clinically accurate southpaw, Hagler was born in Newark on 23 May 1952, one of six children left fatherless when Robert Sims deserted Ida Mae Hagler. The riots persuaded her to seek a safer environment and the family moved to Brockton, Massachusetts, birthplace of Rocky Marciano.

As an amateur, Hagler won all but two of 50 contests and in 1973 became the National AAU middleweight champion, schooled by Pat and Goody Petronelli, brothers from an Italian neighbourhood who operated the best gymnasium in Brockton. It is to Hagler's credit that he

Marvin Hagler, one of the truly great middleweight champions, was paid more than 20 million dollars to defend the undisputed title against Sugar Ray Leonard in 1987. Leonard confounded the odds to gain a controversial points decision at Caesar's Palace in Las Vegas.

remained loyal to the Petronellis, continuing to seek and accept their counsel during a bleak period when alignment with one of the major promotional forces in the United States would have been instantly advantageous.

In return for his cut (30 per cent if a world title is at stake), the manager wheels and deals and goes to the corner in the intervals between rounds with encouragement and advice, wiping away the sweat, cleaning away the blood, but the partnership can never be equal because only one of them is taking the blows.

Barry McGuigan, the most conspicuous of modern Irish heroes, formed a prosperous alliance with Barney Eastwood, a leading Belfast bookmaker, and the partnership seemed to be complete when McGuigan defeated Eusebio Pedroza to become the World Boxing Association featherweight champion. But amidst the euphoria there were flickers of unrest, doubts gathering into mistrust, reminding us that in sport no more sensitive union exists than the one between a fighter and his manager.

When Jim Watt won the lightweight title, it helped to establish Terry Lawless as the most successful manager in British boxing history, but not before falling out with the first of his four world champions, the welterweight John H. Stracey.

No such problems threatened to invade Hagler's relationship with the Petronelli brothers and his faith in them and Steve Wainwright, a lawyer brought in to negotiate contracts, was rewarded with more than $40 million in gross ring earnings. Outside the heavyweight division, only Ray Leonard has made more from boxing, but by comparison with the 1976 Olympic gold medallist, who was astutely packaged as a coming champion from the moment he turned professional, Hagler had to struggle for recognition.

It had not been uncommon for an outstandingly talented boxer to engage in upwards of 50 contests before achieving recognition as a leading contender (Sugar Ray Robinson first won the welterweight championship in his seventy-sixth professional bout), but divided authority, the introduction of bastard weights and television's eagerness to show championships led to a spurious proliferation of titles, short-circuiting the process by which men reached the top in boxing.

With this in mind, Hagler's frustration was understandable. Losses to Bobby Watts and Willie Monroe in the early months of 1976, avenged later by knock-outs, may have fuelled the curious suspicion that he lacked the will to come through as a champion, but doubts certainly existed and he was kept waiting a further three years.

Hagler's chance finally came in Las Vegas on 30 November 1979 when he was matched with Vito Antuofermo, who had outpointed Hugo Corro of Argentina in Monte Carlo six months earlier to win the middleweight title. Antuofermo, born in Italy, fully represented the immigrant dream. He learned to box in a New York Police Department gymnasium and, taking advantage of dual nationality, held the European light-middleweight championship until beaten by Maurice Hope. Antuofermo's record showed 50 professional contests and most of them could be found on his battered and scarred face. Hagler was expected to expose the champion's limited technique, but he boxed cautiously at a critical stage of the contest and the result was a draw.

The challenger was fully entitled to a rematch but found himself cast aside again when the World Boxing Council nominated Alan Minter. Giving the best performance of his career, Minter outboxed Antuofermo in Las Vegas and then cut him up in eight rounds at

Hagler on high after successfully defending the middleweight title against Mustafa Hamsho in 1984.

Canon

Wembley. Now Hagler had to travel across the Atlantic knowing the only way he could beat Minter in London was to destroy him. In doing so he experienced the worst crowd disturbance British boxing has ever known.

Clive Gammon, a Welshman employed as a senior writer by the American magazine *Sports Illustrated*, described it thus:

The most explosive opening round in Championship history. Marvelous Marvin Hagler staggers Thomas Hearns when defending the undisputed middleweight title in Las Vegas on 16 April 1985.

> At close to midnight last Saturday, at Bailey's Hotel in London, Marvin Hagler, the new undisputed middleweight champion of the world, grinned hugely and then pulled on a pint mug of English ale. Only now, and slowly, was he beginning to relax from a frightening experience. Somewhat more than an hour earlier, just after Hagler had taken the title from England's Alan Minter in slightly less than nine blood-bespattered minutes of fighting, exultation had abruptly changed to terror as the ugliest crowd ever to show up at Wembley Arena – 10,000 strong, many high on booze and crude chauvinism – viciously turned on the visiting Americans and their champion.

Plastic beer bottles, many half-full, rained down on the ring and a horrible sound flooded the arena. Police moved in and Hagler's handlers, forming a protective screen above and around their man, led him to safety. As they left in a limousine, a mob chanted the obscene racist slogans of the National Front. Back at the hotel, Hagler made it clear he would never fight in London again.

After seven title defences in which he accommodated a variety of styles without once being seriously threatened or even taken the distance, Hagler was entitled to unanimous recognition, but doubts persisted and gained fresh impetus when Roberto Duran, a triple

KRONK

franklin
SUGAR
RAY

The victors but only one winner. Sugar Ray Leonard and Marvin Hagler wait for the judges' verdict.

April 1987 . . . Hagler was controversially outpointed by Sugar Ray Leonard.

champion, went the full 15 rounds on 30 November 1983, in Las Vegas. Even allowing for Duran's militant refusal to be overwhelmed, Hagler's reluctance to try and dominate the latter part of the contest was a strange manifestation of his darker mood. He had still to provide unassailable proof of genuine greatness.

An opportunity came in April 1985 when Hagler defended against Thomas 'The Hit Man' Hearns, the light-middleweight champion from Detroit and a product of the famous Kronk Gymnasium.

As Hagler stood waiting for the opening bell, he threw short punches upwards at his shaven head, an appropriately aggressive gesture in view of what was to come. When the first round ended, there was a brief moment of stunned silence then a thunderous roar. No witness could recall a more explosive start to a title fight. Both men had struck tremendous blows and the Petronellis worked feverishly in the corner to repair a nasty gash between Hagler's eyes. But though another cut – this time under the right eye – became a problem for the champion, he cut loose again and stopped Hearns in the third round. Now there was no denying his stature.

Almost exactly two months later, Hagler found himself back in the same arena at Caesar's Palace in Las Vegas facing Sugar Ray Leonard, who had been lured out of retirement by a guarantee of $11 million and another chance to satisfy his exaggerated ego. Including a percentage of television profits, Hagler grossed more than $25 million but lost his titles on the closest of split decisions, with Leonard exhausted at the end of 12 thrilling rounds. In many people's eyes Hagler had been wronged again, but his place in boxing history was assured. ■

nklin

Winter comes to Cape Cod, Massachusetts, the perfect setting for Marvin Hagler and an ominous sign for Tony Sibson who was stopped in the ninth round when challenging for the Middleweight Championship in 1983.

SUGAR RAY LEONARD

Like all important memories, a fighter's best days return in rich patches of gold, blinding him to reality, persuading him that the calendar can be kept at bay. For all fighters it is but an ephemeral experience and in that respect they are cursed. Boxing is what they do best, defining them in life, and they find it difficult to let go. 'I came back for this one special fight,' Sugar Ray Leonard stated emphatically after gaining a remarkable, if controversial, decision over Marvelous Marvin Hagler for the World Boxing Council middleweight championship at Caesar's Palace in Las Vegas on 6 April 1987. 'I won it. There is nothing left to prove. I'm through.'

Leonard was not through. Intelligent, articulate, astute, commercially successful, heavly invested, rich beyond anything he could have imagined when growing to manhood in Palmer Park, Maryland, he still found the mysterious thrill irresistible. 'Instinct is making me fight again,' he said. 'How many more? I can't tell. I'm not thinking years, only fights. Of course there is a limit but there is a limit to life. I'd like to box every four or five months until this thing burns out. But fighting remains the ultimate definition of who I am. Then there is a vanity and pride. Everybody has an ego but a fighter's is more exaggerated.'

Returning to Las Vegas in November 1988, Leonard knocked out Donny Lalonde, an enthusiastic but limited Canadian, to become the WBC champion at light-heavyweight and super-middleweight and, uniquely, a title-holder in five separate divisions. But the reality was something that Muhammad Ali and Larry Holmes chose to ignore until they were embarrassed by lesser men. From their seats in a makeshift arena raised over the tennis courts behind Caesar's Palace, the scene of Leonard's resurrection 18 months earlier, they saw it in the anxiety that invaded his eyes after being struck down in the fourth round and the

Hit me if you can. Sugar Ray Leonard employs extravagant tactics to frustrate Marvin Hagler. Referee Richard Steele is puzzled, Hearne unsure. Did Leonard do enough to justify the scoring, winning the Middleweight Championship on a split decision?

Mirror, mirror on the wall, who is the fairest of us all? Sugar Ray Leonard reflects in the public gaze.

desperate manoeuvres he was forced to employ, until taking ferocious advantage of an opportunity to end the contest.

There was such clear evidence of diminished powers that, at 32, permanent retirement ought to have been more than a vague consideration and yet, in February 1989, Leonard signed to fight Thomas Hearns eight years after they came together for the welterweight championship. Hearns, though younger by two years, had begun to display even more alarming signs of accelerating decay: his speech was slurred and he could no longer be relied on to withstand heavy blows to the head.

In the absence of financial imperatives, their complicity in an event made instantly squalid by an overkill of tasteless hyperbole was disturbing. Certainly Leonard had cause to acknowledge the perils. In 1982, while training for a fight with Roger Stafford, he stepped back in pain after taking a thumb in the left eye. A detached retina was diagnosed and he underwent surgery at the John Hopkins Hospital in Baltimore. Modern techniques have eliminated hazard's associated with the injury and Leonard was assured he could continue boxing without risk to his vision. He chose to retire, but the hunger to win, born deep within a man, still possessed Leonard and, though it had also been necessary to bond the retina of his other eye, he came back against Kevin Howard in Worcester, Massachusetts, on 11 May 1984.

As Leonard had not fought for 27 months, errors of judgement and timing were understandable, but there was something altogether more ominous in the way he drew his head back from the line of retaliatory fire when attempting to press home attacks. In the fourth round, Howard countered with a right and Leonard went down for the first time in his professional boxing career. He got up quickly, improved and

The Hit Man, Thomas Hearns, five times a champion and one of the most devastating punchers of all time. Right, a disconsolate Hearns watches Leonard celebrate.

eventually stopped Howard in the ninth; then came the shock. 'I knew even before the knockdown it was over for me,' he said. 'In the first round I tried to establish a rhythm; I tried moving. But when it didn't come, I said "Damn, I'm in trouble." I kept trying to get my hands to work, but they never did. He'd throw a jab, I'd see it coming – and it would hit me. And my right hand was stuttering. It wasn't *my* right hand.'

Ray Charles Leonard (he was named after the singer Ray Charles) was born, one of six brothers and sisters in Wilmington, North Carolina, on 17 May 1956. He took up boxing seriously after the family moved to Palmer Park, a black Maryland suburb close to Washington.

There was an impression of genius in his natural quickness of hand and foot and he rose to prominence during the Montreal Olympics of 1976. 'That kid is as sweet as sugar,' said Tom 'Sarge' Johnson, an assistant coach to the United States team. The description blossomed into a name when Leonard, his virtuosity an arousing feature of the Games, won six bouts in 13 days to take the light-welterweight gold medal.

Even as a momentous future was being predicted, Leonard announced his retirement; he intended to take up the offer of a scholarship to the University of Maryland, study for a business degree and ride the tidal wave of media attention for endorsements and television commercials. The plan might have worked but economic reality conspired against it. When Leonard's parents were taken seriously ill and his girl-friend, Juanita Wilkinson, applied for welfare subsidy to support their 3-year-old son, he turned back to boxing.

Janks Morton, who helped train Leonard, introduced him to Mike Trainer, a Maryland attorney, and their alliance became the most

Leonard lures Hagler in – watched by actress Joan Collins who is gagged by the middle rope.

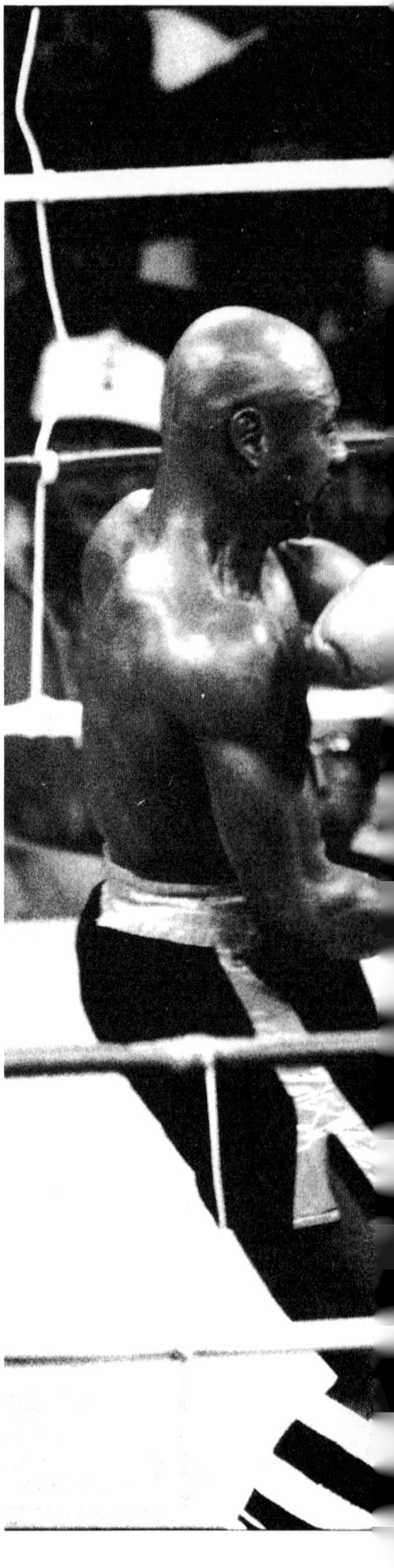

productive in the sport. Trainer knew little about boxing, but 24 friends and business associates were persuaded to invest $20,000 at 8 per cent interest. Leonard repaid them within four years.

The responsibility for choosing Leonard's opponents was given to Angelo Dundee, who had performed a similar role in the formative years of Muhammad Ali's career.

Leonard was paid a phenomenal $40,000 when making his professional début against Luis Vega in Baltimore on 5 February 1977. He won all his 25 contests before stopping Wilfred Benitez in the fifteenth round to become the World Boxing Council welterweight champion.

The two contests against Duran, and particularly the remarkable come-back against Hagler, established Leonard as a truly great champion and by 1989 he was thought to have grossed $90 million from boxing alone. 'Wanting to fight is inexplicable,' he said. 'People's perception of the American way of life is to have a family, a couple of kids and a nice car. That's supposed to be the ultimate. I have all these things and more, so why am I fighting? As a kid I fought to belong. There was no other way to the limelight from my background and education. Now I fight because it makes me happy.' The embers still glowed.

Sophistication is not what we have come to associate with the selling of prize fights, but Bob Arum who brought Leonard and Hearns together again managed to exceed even the monumental standards of crassness set in Las Vegas. The promotional theme, as conveyed on video screens in the Caesar's Palace casino, was death and destruction: exploding bombs, invading armies, atomic eruptions; a mountain of bad taste and utterly offensive.

Franklin

They boxed a draw on 12 June 1989 and I wrote this for *The Independent*:

They embraced on a podium in the Sports Pavilion behind Caesar's Palace close to where a draw was announced after 12 hard rounds and you could tell that Thomas Hearns no longer felt diminished by the presence of Sugar Ray Leonard.

A lot of people were intent on proclaiming him a winner, Leonard a loser, but equality was enough for Hearns. 'I answered a lot of questions,' he shouted excitedly, high on fulfilment and pride, the phrases gushing from him like never before.

Responding theatrically to applause he laid a hand against his face and thrust a foot onto the table-top. 'My chin, the ol' legs. They are still in working condition, and I owe it all to Him up there.' Then glancing across at Leonard, he said: 'Next time, Ray, don't fight me so hard, baby.'

There was already talk of a next time and it filled some of us with despair, because for all the tension they generated as darkness came to what was left of another ferociously hot day in the Nevada desert, Leonard and Hearns are spent fighters who should abandon all thoughts of returning to the ring.

To speak of it as a great fight was to ignore the erosions of time, enthusiastic comparison with their first encounter in 1981 made spurious by unavoidable evidence of accelerating deterioration.

The years have finally caught up with Leonard and though Hearns went frustratingly close to winning the contest, he will never again achieve the emotional peak that almost enabled him to pull off a remarkable upset.

Instead he was persuaded to prove absolute authority over Roberto

Duran going in against the Panamanian for the third time on 9 December 1989.

After 12 exceedingly boring rounds behind the Mirage Hotel in Las Vegas Leonard was still the World Boxing Council super-middleweight champion. This pleased his friends and relatives, loyal employees, enthusiastic supporters, gamblers who took him at odds-on and reporters from various international locations whose judgement survived the groundswell of sentiment that helped to explain why Duran had become a cult figure by the time he arrived in his corner on a chilly night in the Nevada desert.

The scent of cordite left by a spectacular and prolonged explosion of fireworks that burst above the arena, seemed entirely appropriate to the occasion, but by the sixth round there was little left for Duran, the suspicion that he had given his last memorable performance against Iran Barkley nine months earlier, borne out by Leonard's clear superiority.

The 38 year-old challenger was at least expected to go out on his shield, a warrior until the end. Instead he went miserably, utterly outclassed, losing 10 of the rounds, complaining afterwards that Richard Steele, the referee, had prevented him from making a fight of it.

Duran withstood a storm that raged around his head in the 6th round but there was nothing in his legs and not even the sight of blood trickling down the left side of Leonard's face in the 11th round or the crowd's bawling response to a wound, could inspire a decisive effort. 'If this was the last time there will be no announcement,' Leonard said. 'But I didn't look as old as you all felt I was.' It was time for them both to bid us farewell. ■

JOHNNY OWEN

Before Michael Spinks went to his corner to face Gerry Cooney for an ersatz version of the heavyweight championship in Atlantic City on 15 June 1987, he indicated an acute awareness of the hazards that exist in the ring. 'It's a life threat,' said the former Olympic gold medallist who retired twelve months later after being devastated in 91 seconds by Mike Tyson. 'I'm telling you, what I do for a living can be terrifying.'

Opponents of professional boxing, particularly people whose objections spring from medical rather than moral grounds, have a substantial case and even those of us who continue to find the hard old game irresistibly thrilling are obliged to accept that it is fraught with the ultimate peril.

According to the revised edition of Maurice Golesworthy's Encyclopaedia of Boxing, *close to 400 fatalities world-wide have resulted from injuries sustained in the ring during the last five decades, an average of between eight and nine a year, and despite improved safeguards (The World Boxing Council shortened championship bouts to 12 rounds following the death of Deuk-Koo Kim, a South Korean lightweight, in November 1982), there remains a disturbing sense of inevitable tragedy.*

Whether this strengthens the argument against boxing is a matter for individual conscience; but even people who stubbornly refuse to concede that professional fighters are at least risking irreparable damage to their brain cells found themselves on dangerous ground when Johnny Owen died in a coma seven weeks after being knocked out in the twelfth round by Lupe Pintor at the Olympic Auditorium in Los Angeles on 19 September 1980.

As Owen, a 24-year-old from Merthyr Tydfil, held the European title and had lost only one of 26 professional contests by the time he came to challenge Pintor for the World Boxing Council bantamweight championship, it was thought to be a legitimate match, despite the understandable apprehension felt by some of the Welshman's compatriots.

Their anxiety stemmed not only from experience of the violence that comes naturally to Mexican fighters and the knowledge that Pintor, squat and powerful, was by far the more seasoned man (with a record of 41 victories and seven defeats), but also from the alarming impression of frailty Owen conveyed whenever he climbed into his corner: looking so thin and pale that people seeing him for the first time were inclined to prepare themselves for a harrowing experience.

The concern for Owen's safety increased when it was announced that he would not be leaving for Los Angeles until a week before the fight, a misguided decision in view of the difficulties imposed by an eight-hour time difference. It is impossible to determine how much this affected Owen's performance, but after holding his own through the early rounds (Mickey Duff, the London promoter and matchmaker had them level at the half-way stage), he began to wilt, coming

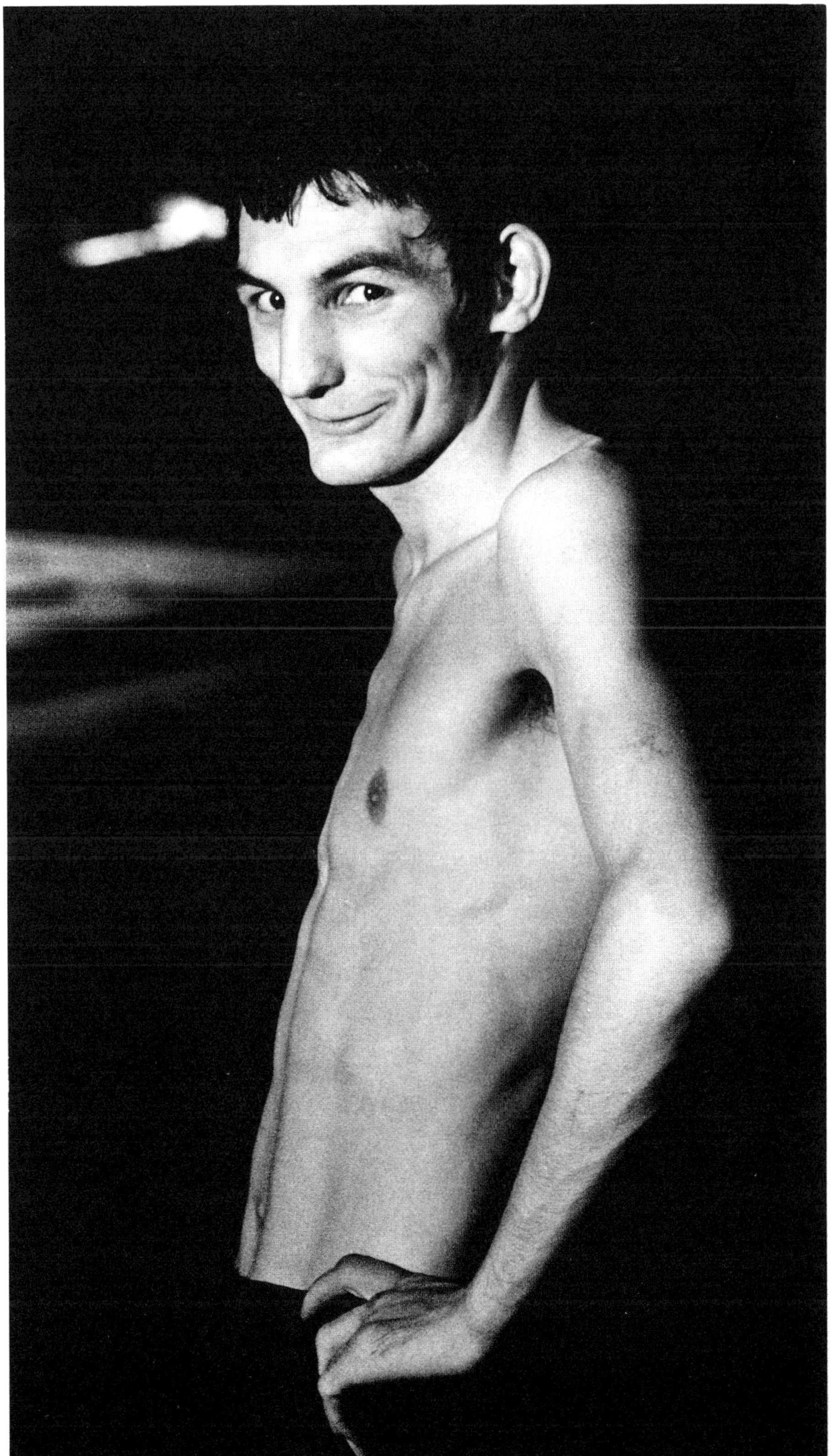

The Matchstick Man. Johnny Owen before he challenged Lupe Pintor of Mexico for the World Bantamweight Championship in Los Angeles on 19 September 1980. The Welshman from Merthyr Tydfil became one of the most tragic figures in modern boxing when he died as a result of injuries sustained during the contest.

under such heavy fire that only an immense will kept him in the contest. With just 40 seconds of the twelfth round left, the terrible drama began to develop. A short right sent Owen to his knees and after a mandatory count he was driven to the other side of the ring and there took a savage right. The blow hurled Owen backwards and his head thudded against the floor of the ring. He died after lingering in a coma for seven weeks.

* * * * *

Early snow had settled upon the hills around Merthyr as though nature had sent a shroud for Johnny Owen; the valley had not forgotten how to dress for sadness: clouds grey and forlorn, the white flakes dissolving into grimy dampness on the streets of the town.

Johnny Owen had come home the previous night, up through Rhymney and Tredegar, over Dowlais top and then down to rest in a church at the bottom of the town.

Their bedside vigil over, Dick and Edith Owen brought their son back to his people, travelling slowly through those little places where the following for him had been strongest.

It was easy to think of Johnny Owen's death as another of the tragedies Merthyr seemed destined to endure. Of all the towns in the world, none seems better prepared for mourning. And in the brief flicker of life, he surely sensed the resilience that prevails there.

Merthyr never quite took to Johnny Owen's boxing. He fought mostly on the other side of the hill and it was only in death that his heroism was fully celebrated. 'This is a tough town,' said an old man. 'People became hard because they had to be. That is part of Merthyr's heritage. We mourn Johnny Owen like we mourned all those poor children who died at Aberfan. And yet I sense that the valley is conditioned to such things.'

The chapels and churches preached that the meek would inherit the earth. But under oppressive iron-masters and mine owners, the people learned how to scuffle, to scrap, to master the grim strategies of survival.

'Aye, it's been a hard place right enough,' said Eddie Thomas, the former British and European welterweight champion. 'So hard that Al Capone would have struggled to make a crust peddling papers. It was always a fighting town. "Fight me by here? Aye, I'll fight you." Happened to me many times. Got a few beltings, but you learn, don't you?'

Johnny Owen learned. He was not as gifted as Howard Winstone, who brought the world featherweight championship back to Merthyr. But he worked at his boxing. He ran and ran over the steep hills, achieving stamina remarkable in such a slight frame; a painfully shy boy transformed in the ring.

Thomas was forced to question his own involvement in boxing as a manager and promoter when he heard of Owen's death and again when he saw him lying in a coffin at Gatwick Airport. 'You ask yourself whether it is worth going on, whether there is any sense in it. But then it comes to you. Boxing isn't simply about establishing an identity or making money. It is mostly about a mysterious thrill. Why did Joe Frazier want to fight again when he was already a millionaire? The roar of the crowd? Not just that, but knowing that all those cheering people are living something through you. It was in me as it was in Johnny Owen.'

A sport which requires men to render each other senseless is bound to be vulnerable, but in a truly civilized world there would be no famine or the threat of global vaporization.

We stood shoulder to shoulder in a chapel and sang the old hymns and then climbed the hill to where a brave fighter was laid to rest; thousands lining the funeral route: the women tearful and twisting hankies tight against strained faces, the men solemn and bareheaded.

There are more serious issues at stake than the validity of prize-fighting and as I stood at the graveside there was some comfort in the belief that Johnny Owen understood why some of us would be at the ringside again. ■

BARRY McGUIGAN

One of the most thrilling episodes in the modern history of British boxing came to a bloodied conclusion in Manchester on 31 May 1989 when Barry McGuigan announced his retirement from the ring after being stopped in the fourth round by Jim McDonnell, a caretaker from Camden Town in London, who had not been thought capable of interrupting the Irishman's advance towards another world title.

It was a wise decision. The defeat resulted from a long thin cut near McGuigan's right eye, but he had never looked thoroughly convincing since beginning a come-back in April 1988 and it soon became clear that he could no longer generate the exuberant intensity that excited audiences on both sides of the Irish Sea.

So ended a career that reached its zenith on a night of great Celtic jubilation at the Queens Park Rangers football ground in June 1985, when McGuigan took the World Boxing Association featherweight champion from Eusebio Pedroza of Panama.

* * * * *

My friend was persistent. 'You should come over and have a look at this boy,' he said. 'You'll like him. Fast hands, big heart. He's fighting next week.'

Belfast. Road blocks and patrols. 'Send the kids over to me until things calm down,' I had said. Those children were now grown but there was no end to the trouble.

I took my seat at the Ulster Hall, nodding to acquaintances, marvelling at their cheerful resilience.

Barry McGuigan from Clones; a gold medallist at the Commonwealth Games in 1978. On the other side of the card it said, Peter Eubanks, Brighton. Fighting for the sixth time as a professional, McGuigan was seeking revenge for a points defeat and when he came to the ring I remembered: a pale, busy kid winning at Wembley on the night Alexis Arguello took the world lightweight championship from Jim Watt.

It was all over in the eighth and McGuigan was on his way, a polite young man who spoke respectfully to his manager, Barney Eastwood, the Belfast bookmaker who would take him to a world title. A famous Irish alliance, it prospered mightily at the King's Hall, Belfast, and when, after a string of tumultuously received victories, McGuigan defeated Pedroza, many thought he was a true genius of the game. Two defences and then Las Vegas.

Hugh McIlvanney of the *Observer* agreed that it was worth deserting the World Cup for a couple of days and we left Mexico City early on the morning of 23 June 1986, reaching Las Vegas in plenty of time to see Steve Cruz, a Texan from Fort Worth, challenge for McGuigan's championship at Caesar's Palace.

There was nothing in Cruz's record to suggest that McGuigan was approaching a

**Only the beginning.
Barry McGuigan celebrating
a gold medal at
the Commonwealth Games
in Edmonton.**

crisis, but as the contest progressed in a suffocating 120° F, he began to experience such withering distress that by the bell there was nothing left but gameness: the title had gone.

McGuigan did not fight again for 22 months and by February 1986 what had been Barry and Barney was McGuigan versus Eastwood, no more than a case to be heard in a Belfast courtroom: the most conspicuous of modern Irish heroes attempting to prove that there was nothing to come for the Belfast bookmaker.

There was, it seemed, plenty still to come from McGuigan, a projected come-back at 9 st 4 lb, which is why the bitterness that had invaded their relationship was being aired again, with Eastwood claiming that a settlement reached the previous year gave him promotional rights to McGuigan's next two contests.

'I didn't concede anything,' declared McGuigan. 'I got what I was owed.'

With Frank Warren, the London promoter as his manager, McGuigan expected to be back in the ring within two months, attempting to obliterate the memory of his ordeal in the Nevada desert, claiming that his state of mind had been more of a disadvantage than the debilitating heat.

'I shouldn't have gone in there,' he said. 'Sure the heat was a problem, but it didn't matter as much as the way I felt coming up to the fight. It was what I saw when Lloyd Honeyghan lost to Jorge Vaca. Looking at Lloyd I saw myself in Las Vegas. Nothing, just not the same man.'

It was after watching Honeyghan concede to mental dishevelment, when losing the World Boxing Council welterweight championship, that McGuigan decided to box again. He had thought about it, agonized over it, frequently recalling the misgivings expressed by his father, Pat, whose death was the source of a deep and abiding sadness that could still bring tears to his eyes.

The moisture came to them again when McGuigan was driving home with Tony Clarke, then his business manager, from a fight between Tony Sibson and Brian Anderson. 'We stopped for a cup of tea so that Barry could compose himself,' Clarke recalled, 'and for a while he was very quiet. Then he looked at me and said he fancied boxing again. He does not have to because things are going well in all sorts of directions and Barry is looking at a substantial future. But that is what is in him and it's better to do it than go on thinking about it. I wasn't sure and perhaps Barry wasn't, but the Honeyghan fight changed all that. I knew then that he wanted to be back in the ring.'

McGuigan had abandoned thoughts of boxing at 9 stone, the weight at which he appeared to be unstoppable until opponents discovered that he was not the same man when

Drained by the desert heat Barry McGuigan loses his WBA featherweight championship to Steve Cruz in Las Vegas, 23 June 1986.

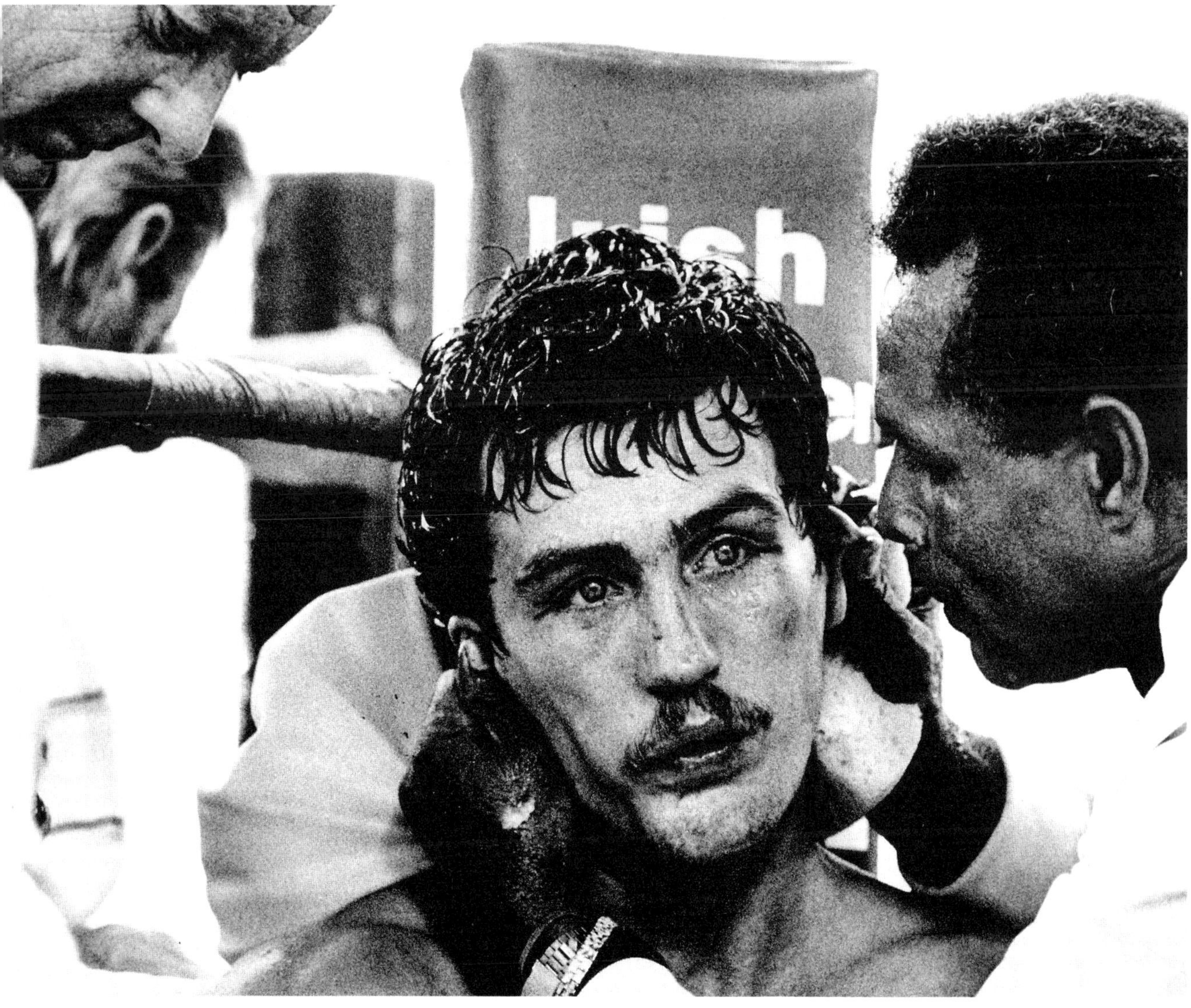

boxing on the retreat. 'It was a real struggle down from 9 st 2 lb,' he said, confirming old suspicions. 'I would diet and find myself at 8 st 12 lb. Off the diet and straight back to where I had been. Never comfortable. Now I'm around 9 st 9 lb and I'll make 9 st 4 lb easily.'

He had moved to a village 12 miles from Milton Keynes in Buckinghamshire, the location convenient for the airports in Birmingham and Luton, business appointments in London and, significantly, the motor-racing circuit at Silverstone. He remained eager to establish a reputation in sports cars and according to Clarke possessed the talent to develop into an outstanding driver. 'As long as he leaves the devil's horns at home, I can see that for him,' he said. 'He's good, but a bit reckless. One shunt towards the end of last year really worried me.'

No less worrying was the thought that McGuigan was not responding entirely to whatever mysterious instinct persuades retired boxers back into the ring. Was he doing it for an even more perilous reason, to project his commercial potential further?

When brought forward by Eastwood in those days when they appeared to be as close as most fathers and sons, McGuigan looked a natural, his zest for the game complete and unimpaired, his triumphs transcending the sectarian differences that persist so horribly in Northern Ireland. The years had slipped by and McGuigan could not be sure that the old desire was still with him. 'For a long time I didn't go near boxing,' he said. 'I ran but that was all. I knew that if I went to the gym I would see my father, there but no longer there. Facing up to that was difficult. I've been through some bad times since Las Vegas and when things broke up with Barney I didn't want any badness. I thought we could settle matters. But here we go again.' Once it was never Barney, always Mr Eastwood.

It is not enough to be back with the running, the sparring and the slap of a rope, to know once again those fierce disciplines required of fighting men: to know the truth about himself a fighter must fight.

McGuigan sought the truth when he faced Nicky Perez, the North American super-featherweight champion at the Alexandra Pavilion in north London on 20 April 1988. Despite the hours of dedicated preparation, the 150 rounds of sparring and the admiration expressed by those who had watched him at work, McGuigan couldn't be sure. 'It takes time to clear the head,' he said in his dressing-room. 'This fight will tell me a lot; another fight will tell me more. But if I sense that it is all a mistake, then I'll not be wasting people's time. I'll be out of there.'

Even during his great days, there was a suspicion that McGuigan's technical shortcomings might be exploited by an

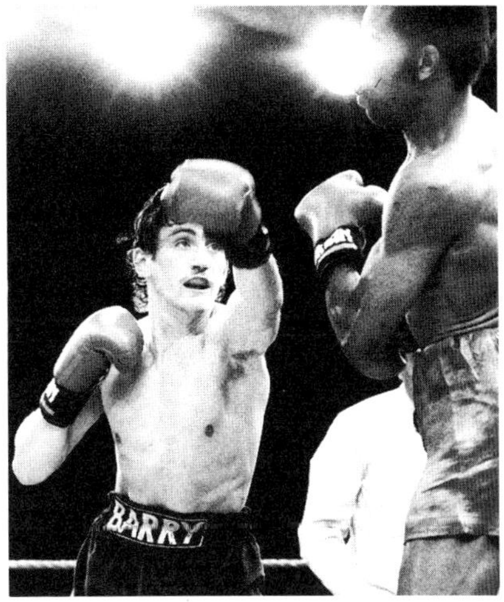

On a night of great Celtic jubilation in London, Barry McGuigan defeats Eusebio Pedroza on 8 June 1985 to become the WBA World Featherweight Champion.

opponent as gifted but younger than Pedroza. The ferocity of his attacks, the momentum he built up, concealed a weakness, the difficulty he experienced when trying to box on the retreat, and because of an impetuous tendency to deliver left hooks to the body along a flat trajectory, he could be caught with right counters.

Cruz, who subsequently lost the title to Antonio Esparragoze of Venezuela, took full advantage of those flaws in Las Vegas, pressing forward in response to excited urging from his corner.

Perez, a Mexican boxing out of Tucson, Arizona, was not thought to be a problem. He had lost 16 of 75 professional contests since turning professional at 17, three of those defeats by world champions: Wilfredo Gomez, Salvador Sanchez and Julio Cesar Chavez. At 28, he was probably well past his best; the fight lasted four rounds.

The euphoria that filled McGuigan's dressing-room survived the night in between and when he came to speak about beating Perez, the past and the future, hopes and fears, his eyes were bright with elation. Nobody understood the mood better than his wife Sandra, pregnant with their fourth child and experiencing again the anxiety of being married to a fighter. 'I was so nervous,' she said, 'then the music started and when I heard the cheers for Barry, I cried.'

Twenty-two months earlier, she had prayed while worried men hovered around her husband's prone form, their concern so devastatingly real that the nightmare was still tucked away in a corner of her mind. 'It came flooding back at the ringside and for two rounds I couldn't bear to look,' she said. 'I thought Barry had done enough in boxing and if it had been up to me, he would not be going through this all over again. But that would be unfair and there is a buzz in him now that I haven't sensed for a long while. It's better this way than to hear him say in a few years that he was wrong not to do it.'

The doing of it had banished most of the understandable apprehension from McGuigan's mind, most obviously the possibility that he could no longer rely on the impulses that took him to the featherweight championship. The timing had not always been there and he felt that it was necessary to do some work on his jab. 'It isn't quite what it was and I could have been more composed,' he said. 'If you don't have that, you get knocked on your arse.'

Two months later, McGuigan stopped Francisco Tomas Cruz in four rounds and was then matched with Julio Miranda of Argentina. As the World Boxing Council, an organization notorious for generous assessments, rated 17 men above Miranda in the 9 st 4 lb division, McGuigan appeared to be marking time while negotiations proceeded for a championship fight. 'We've been moving towards it since Barry decided to box again and if things work out, he can start thinking about Azumah Nelson,' said Frank Warren.

Nelson, the crafty and powerful Ghanaian who destroyed Pat Cowdell in one round when they met for the WBC championship in 1985, lurked in McGuigan's consciousness.

No bad things could be imagined when McGuigan went to his corner against an opponent whose record showed only one knockout, but what was thought to be a routine warm-up developed into one of the most difficult fights of his career.

When the referee, Larry O'Connell, stepped between them after 75 seconds of the eighth round, McGuigan was cut above both eyes and had been required to reach deep into the well in order to subdue a resourceful and wily opponent. McGuigan had won again but with no conviction. His supporters were encouraged to believe they would soon be celebrating a more substantial victory, but there was an alternative point of view and it related to the suspicion that while McGuigan thrilled to the prospect of another title, his responses were no longer those of a natural fighting man.

In order not to be misunderstood and to establish the credentials of a fighting man, let me relate a tale about Judah Bergman, better known as Jack 'Kid' Berg, the Whitechapel Windmill, who became junior welterweight champion of the world. Berg, now 80, was trained in the United States by Ray Arcel, who celebrated his ninetieth birthday in 1988.

Arcel's pet name for Berg was Yitzel. One night when crouching in Berg's corner, Arcel winced as the little Londoner came under heavy fire, taking blow after blow to the body. Whenever Berg gasped, Arcel groaned. Still fighting back when the bell sounded to end the round, Berg did a smart about-turn and strode briskly back to his corner.

'Yitzel!' said Arcel, his voice heavy with concern. 'Yitzel, how do you feel?'

'Fine, thank you,' replied Berg. 'And you?'

It could be assumed that McGuigan had not expressed a similar sentiment when his cornermen enquired anxiously about his health, finding it necessary to repair torn brows and develop a strategy to account for an opponent who would surely have made a greater impact in the division if his gifts had included the ability to deliver concussive blows.

There was a time when the little Irishman might have revelled in the problems, brushing them aside with the concentrated assaults that established him as one of the most excitingly combative figures to emerge in British boxing for many years.

The cuts apart, McGuigan was never seriously threatened by Miranda, winning all but two of the completed rounds, but when set against the grim threat of heavier artillery, the

On the way back. Barry McGuigan stops Tomas De La Cruz in Luton on 25 June 1988.

performance gave rise to concern.

The future was now blurred by a sense of disenchantment with the rigours of a trade that never fails, one way or another, to take something from them all. Drama is essential stuff for heroes and it helps to explain why boxing history is littered with tales of good men who did not perceive the passing of their time in the ring.

McGuigan's problem appeared to be of a different kind: not an unwillingness to settle for the past tense, but a subconscious rejection of the instinct from which his reputation sprang.

Something similar could be sensed in John Conteh, before he dissolved against Saad Muhammad when attempting to regain the light-heavyweight championship in Atlantic City on 29 March 1980, and if profitable stature was the only motivating force, then McGuigan was on dangerous ground.

There would be no title. McGuigan accepted an offer of £250,000 to fight Jim McDonnell and that was the end of it.

It was as if he had been in rehearsal for the moment and when it came he gave an immaculate performance, never once shedding a tear or trying to avoid the truth, fully aware of his place in boxing history.

The rest of McGuigan's life had only just begun, but he was not diminished by retirement, the valediction delivered firmly with barely a pause for breath. 'I would like to apologize and thank everyone who has supported me,' he said, perched on a metal bin in the corridor outside a hotel room in Manchester, dressed casually in blue denim slacks and a matching shirt, reaching every now and again to wipe away the perspiration that gathered in small hollows above his moustache. It had come to past tenses and he seemed to be relieved.

Some men approached McGuigan and one of them stepped forward to embrace him. Another career had come to an end and the beaten fighter's children played happily in the background, oblivious to the small drama. A crowd gathered in the lobby down below, chattering excitedly about the night's events.

'Is he all right?' somebody asked out loud. expressing concern for the loser.

'Sure it was an elbow that did the damage,' said a man from across the Irish Sea, attempting to rationalize the defeat.

McGuigan wanted none of that. 'It was a slicing punch,' he said, demonstrating how the heel of McDonnell's left glove had ripped into his brow. 'No complaints.'

That is the way of it. They come and they go, the cheers welling up and then subsiding. The beaten fighter had been in there for the last time. ■

MIKE TYSON

Mike Tyson, who escaped from a New York ghetto to become one of the most remarkable figures in boxing history – Heavyweight Champion at just 21 years old.

By the summer of 1988 Mike Tyson was so completely the world heavyweight champion, so convincingly one of the most dramatic figures ever to inhabit professional boxing, that his excesses were bound to be regarded as conclusive proof of something more potentially terminal than any hazards he could expect to encounter in the ring.

None of the leading contenders for what is unquestionably the richest prize in sport could expect to cope with what Tyson brings to an essentially brutal trade: not only quickness and mobility remarkable in such a powerful man, nor even his devastating hand speed, but above all the controlled ferocity that justifies comparison with the best men who have fought in the heavyweight division.

But even before demolishing Michael Spinks in 91 seconds in Atlantic City, New Jersey, on 27 June 1988, it was clear that Tyson, at just 21, was finding it difficult to cope with important changes in his life; and subsequent controversial happenings suggested that violent adolescent experiences had permanently disfigured his personality.

Within hours of pulverizing Spinks, the champion announced his retirement. And though this was thought to be a strategy, an attempt to invalidate contractual agreements, including a title defence against Frank Bruno, the British heavyweight, it was abundantly obvious that Tyson had reached a crisis in his career.

A thrillingly emphatic victory was achieved despite domestic upheaval and the bitterness that had invaded Tyson's association with Bill Cayton, who had become his sole manager following the death of Jim Jacobs three months earlier. A millionaire from the sale of a family supermarket chain, a world handball champion and notable boxing historian, Jacobs provided an umbilical link with Cus D'Amato, the reclusive trainer and manager who became Tyson's mentor and legal

guardian after persuading him to reject delinquent tendencies formed on the streets of Brownsville, a notorious New York ghetto.

By then, Tyson had married Robin Givens, a television actress and drop-out from the Harvard Medical School. Givens and her mother, Ruth Roper, an astute New York business woman, took control of the champion's affairs, disputing the 30 per cent deducted from all sources by his management team. Jacobs might have held them in check. Cayton, a cold negotiator who could not establish a sound relationship with Tyson, had no chance.

Neither did the marriage. Tyson was seen more frequently back in Harlem, where he damaged a hand in a scuffle with Mitch Green, one of only three men to remain upright against him in the ring. This led to a postponement of the defence against Bruno and it was called off indefinitely when a hospital report revealed that Tyson had been unconscious for 20 minutes following a car accident in the Catskill Mountains outside the home of Camille Ewald, his surrogate mother and D'Amato's sister-in-law.

Rancorous matrimonial exchanges so confused the champion that there was no guarantee he would ever fight again. As there was also plenty of evidence to suggest the reassertion of criminal instincts, Tyson seemed as likely to end up in a penal establishment or on the mortuary slab as the Hall of Fame.

One of three children, Tyson was born on 30 June 1966 in Beford-Stuyvesant, a section of Brooklyn, New York, through which it is advisable to travel by armoured car. Tyson never knew his father and when 10 found himself in Brownsville, an even tougher neighbourhood. 'I guess I'm a street fighter at heart,' he would say after being launched on a professional career, 'but it wasn't always that way. I was raised by

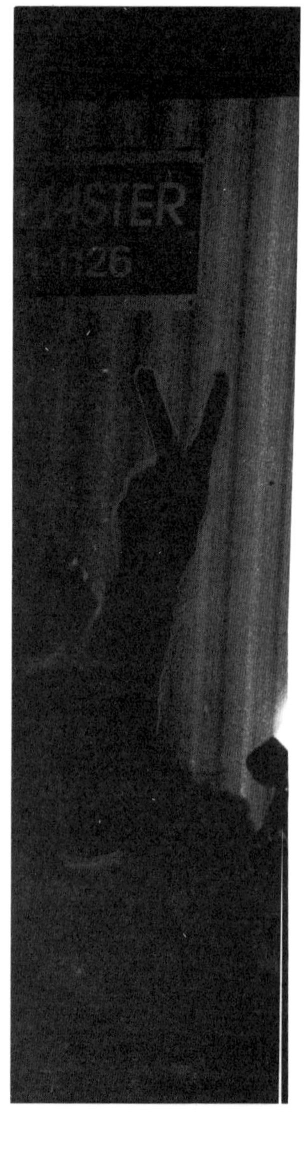

The only one in the frame. Mike Tyson, the reformed delinquent from Brownsville New York, who was thought to be unbeatable, after establishing himself as the undisputed Heavyweight Champion, acknowledges his supporters from the window of a trailer in the car park at Caesar's Palace Las Vegas.

my mother and she hated violence. My brother was five years older than me, so I spent a lot of time with my sister. I picked up my early habits from my mother and sister, really gentle people.'

A different impression was created on the streets. Tyson began to run with hard men, robbing and mugging, and by his thirteenth birthday had been marked down for serious trouble. 'It was crazy stuff,' he said, 'and my mother hated me for it.'

Tyson was sent to the Tryon School, a correction centre in up-state New York, and there learned his basic boxing skills from one of the guards, Bobby Stewart, a former professional fighter. Just before Tyson was due to be paroled, Stewart took him to Cus D'Amato.

D'Amato had been training and counselling young boxers since discovering Floyd Patterson, the former heavyweight champion, in a school for emotionally disturbed boys. Many years earlier, D'Amato had spent an evening with Harold Conrad, a journalist, publicist and pedlar of one-line wisdom who has spent a lifetime around boxing. D'Amato and Patterson had fallen out,

'Cus was low,' Conrad recalled, 'and he began to imagine his ideal heavyweight. Height around five ten. Weight around 218 pounds. Quick footed, fast hands, good puncher, strong chin, determined and mean, receptive and eager to learn. Cus was describing Tyson before the kid was born.'

D'Amato first saw Tyson, then 14, in 1980 when Stewart brought him to a gymasium above the Catskill Police Station. He watched them spar three rounds and then declared: 'That's the heavweight champion. If he wants it, it's his.' The astonishing prophecy was repeated a few days later to Jim Jacobs, who so admired D'Amato's methods and philosophy that he covered the gymnasium overheads.

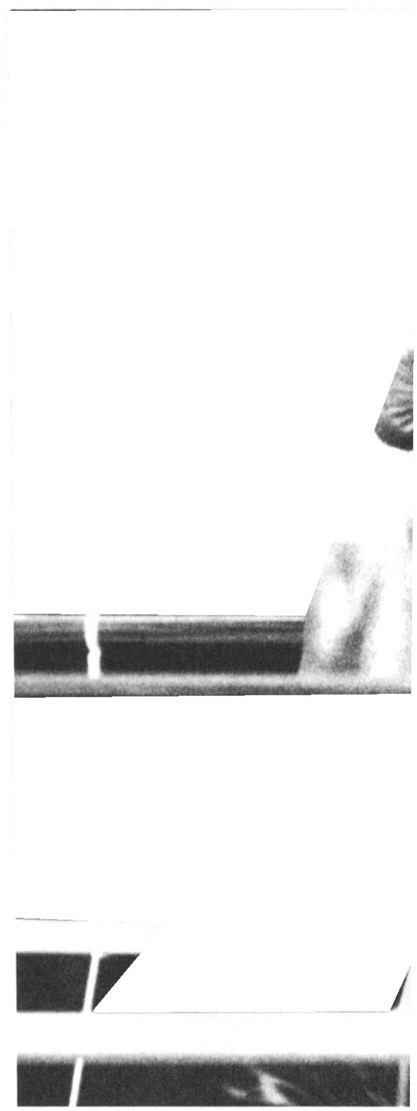

Spoiling tactics enabled James 'Bonecrusher' Smith to get the distance with Mike Tyson.

After obtaining permission to spend a probationary fortnight with D'Amato and his sister-in-law, Tyson moved in permanently. 'In the beginning it was difficult,' Camille recalled, 'Mike was full of rebellion and deeply suspicious and we had to gain his trust.'

Apart from refining Tyson's raw talent in the gymnasium, D'Amato set about improving his mind. From being almost illiterate, the boy responded so well to private tuition that he was soon able to benefit from D'Amato's extensive library. 'If I close my eyes when Tyson speaks I can hear Cus,' Conrad said. 'It's uncanny. The words, the phrases, even the pitch of his voice.'

There are plenty of witnesses who will testify to the progress Tyson made as a fighter, learning to inflict hurt from positions achieved with a swiftness normally associated with much lighter men.

D'Amato preached a style Patterson made famous: a peek-a-boo, hands held high, chin tucked in behind the gloves. Tyson developed a modified version of this, concentrating on the areas D'Amato believed to be vital: the liver, the kidneys, the heart, the vulnerable lower ribs and, of course, the chin. He was also made to appreciate that a fighter must live with peril and pain. 'Cus stressed that there is no difference between a coward and a hero,' he recalled. 'Both experience fear. It is the way a fighter reacts that counts. Cus always wanted to push you, find out what made you work. Then afterwards he would put on a bit more pressure to discover out what would make you break. He said it built character. At the beginning it used to drive me insane and I felt like strangling him. I'd ask why he didn't just spank me instead.'

By 1984 Tyson had progressed sufficiently to be considered for the Olympics, but lost twice in the trials to Henry Tillman. The second of those defeats, a disputed decision in Las Vegas, infuriated D'Amato.

'The head, the heart, the lower ribs, the liver,' emphasized Cus D'Amato when schooling Mike Tyson to become Heavyweight Champion. Tyrell Biggs discovered how well the young New Yorker had learned. No where to go, no point in getting up.' Bottom. The end for Tyrell Biggs as Mike Tyson hovers.

'The Los Angeles Games would have been special for him. It isn't often that they take place in your own country and he would have walked away with the gold medal. Being robbed was a real test of character.'

Tyson fought for the last time as an amateur in September 1984, beating Hakan Brock, a Swede, to win the Tampere International in Finland. Five months later he turned professional and, fighting every three weeks, won 15 in a row: all by knock-out; 11 in the first round. Managed by Jim Jacobs and Bill Cayton, he was soon established as a sensational figure in the division and signed a lucrative four-fight contract with ABC, the American television network.

The impression of destructive force was given further emphasis by Tyson's rejection of familiar appendages. He came to his corner robeless, sockless, wearing plain black shorts and low-cut boots. He looked immediately like one of the old-timers he studies so intently on film and a percussive momentum relates significantly to an appreciation of the great lightweights in history: Benny Leonard, Joe Gans and Roberto Duran. 'Those guys always seemed to know where they were in the ring,' he said. 'Size and style didn't come into it. They just knew how to go about their job.'

On 4 November 1985, D'Amato died of pneumonia. Nine days later, Tyson fought Eddie Richardson in Houston, Texas. 'It is what Cus would have wanted,' Tyson said. 'I shall dedicate each of my victories to the man who meant more to me than anybody I have known.' Twelve months later he was dedicating a championship.

In an attempt to unify a title ludicrously fragmented by self-serving rival boxing commissions, Home Box Office (HBO), the American cable television network, entered into an agreement with Don King and Butch Lewis, two influential promoters. King, a preposterous but

Closer to becoming the undisputed Heavyweight Champion, Mike Tyson in the line of fire after defeating James 'Bonecrusher' Smith for the WBA Heavyweight title.

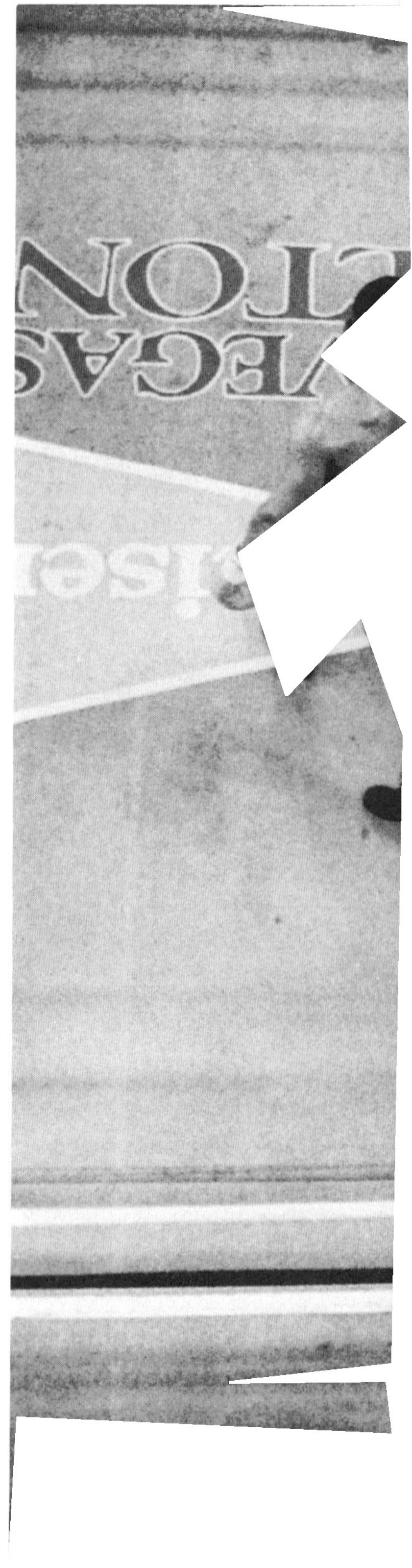

A hero in the moment of truth. Frank Bruno is rescued by the referee, Richard Steele. Mike Tyson stalks to a neutral corner. Bruno's manager, Terry Lawless, waves a white towel in surrender.

undeniably powerful former numbers racketeer from Cleveland, pulled most of the strings in the heavyweight division. Lewis managed Michael Spinks, who took the IBF title from Larry Holmes.

A series of eliminators was meant to culminate in a contest between Spinks and whoever emerged with the World Boxing Council and World Boxing Association championships. The list of contenders did not include Tyson, whose contests were being televised by HBO, but the young New Yorker made such startling progress that he was matched with Trevor Berbick for the WBC title.

Covering that fight for the *Independent*, I wrote: 'By the time Trevor Berbick could see clearly again and the awful clamour had at last gone from his head, Mike Tyson was being proclaimed heavyweight champion of the world.' At 20 years 4 months and 22 days, Tyson had become the youngest heavyweight champion in history.

Comparisons were pointless because the young New Yorker appeared to be unique. It was difficult to imagine that anyone had hit harder at such blinding speed and Berbick lasted just 5 minutes and 37 seconds.

Returning to Las Vegas less than three months later, Tyson took the WBA title from James 'Bonecrusher' Smith. He outpointed Tony Tucker for the vacant IBF title, knocked out Tyrell Biggs, Larry Holmes and Tony Tubbs and then destroyed Michael Spinks in June 1988 to become the undisputed champion.

It was almost eight months before Tyson was seen in the ring again, at last fulfilling an agreement to fight Frank Bruno, a limited but shrewdly promoted British heavyweight whose local reputation had survived an 11th round knockout in July 1986 when challenging Tim Witherspoon for the WBA title.

Budweiser

Could a champion be manufactured from someone who merely looked the part? I wrote the following pieces for The Independent.

* * * * *

Another foe lies stricken. 'The winner by a knock-out . . . Frank Bruno.' Tumult. They chant his name. 'This is the best heavyweight we've ever had,' declares Bruno's manager, Terry Lawless, excitedly. 'Maybe the best in the world.'

Exaggeration is a way of life in professional boxing and it is often difficult to separate fact from fiction, reality from myth; Bruno, the most popular sports personality in Britain, is being paid more than £1.5 million to challenge Mike Tyson for the world heavyweight championship in Las Vegas next Saturday, but the unavoidable conclusion is that he is more myth than reality.

There is nothing in Bruno's record to suggest that he can handle an opponent of Tyson's class, and there are clear impressions of protective matchmaking, relentless lobbying in the higher councils of the game and promotional techniques pioneered by the late Phineas T. Barnum.

Only one British-born heavyweight, Bob Fitzimmons (he arrived in the United States via New Zealand and Australia after leaving Cornwall as a child in 1871), has held the world championship. It is in this historical context, a century of yearning, that we must consider the making of Frank Bruno, and a manufacturing process it certainly has been. Promoters are always on the look-out for a heavyweight and demographic trends made it likely that the next one to emerge in Britain would be black.

Bruno, born in Hammersmith, London, on 16 November 1961, the son of West Indian immigrants, was sent to a corrective school at 11 after striking a teacher. He first attracted attention in the ring at the finals of the South-east Divisional championships in 1980.

He went on to win the national Amateur Boxing Association heavyweight championship and then signed an agreement with Burt McCarthy, a wealthy London business man who was eager to manage him. McCarthy's brother Leslie, now an associate of Frank Warren, the London fight promoter and entrepreneur, said: 'Burt subsidized Bruno, paid him money. He was then approached by Al Hamilton, who claimed to have done a lot for him and wanted a share of his purse money. This was to be paid out of Bruno's percentage but Burt advised against it.'

Hamilton, a sports journalist, is a family friend and the self-styled mentor of Bruno. He took Bruno to Terry Lawless, the most successful manager in British boxing. 'I don't know what Frank is like now,' added McCarthy, 'but in those days he was unpredictable, always changing his mind. Burt

Could a manufactured challenger become the Heavyweight Champion? Frank Bruno in training for his fight with Mike Tyson in Las Vegas on 25 February, 1989.

had lodged the agreement with the British Board of Control but, much to his annoyance, they ruled that Bruno was a free agent.' The Board subsequently accepted a contract from Lawless and McCarthy issued a writ; he received a considerable settlement.

Professional boxing in the United Kingdom is administered by area councils accountable through unpaid stewards to a central authority. Formed in 1929, the Board of Control derives income from a tax levied on promotions and the issue of licences. Boxers' welfare is their paramount responsibility. On 8 October 1980, the Board rejected Bruno's application to box professionally. He was short-sighted in the right eye.

Lawless immediately consulted David McLeod, an opthalmic specialist then working at Moorfields Hospital in London. McLeod recommended delicate surgery that was being performed in the Soviet Union and Colombia. There was no guarantee that the Soviets would issue a visa, so Bruno was referred to Professor José Ignacio Barraquer, who agreed to operate at his clinic in Bogota. 'Bruno was still in touch with us,' added McCarthy, 'and my brother told him not to be obligated, that he would write to Lawless offering to pay for treatment, but nothing came of it.'

In the second week of February 1981, Barraquer scored the surface of Bruno's right eye, making minute incisions. Ten days later, after lonely confinement to a darkened room in a cheap hotel, Bruno learned that the operation had been successful.

It cost Lawless £5,000 but the Board of Control was not convinced and deferred Bruno's case for a further 12 months. Bruno was granted a licence on 10 February 1982. On 12 February the Board accepted a standard contract establishing Lawless as Bruno's manager; the rules allow for managers to receive 25 per cent of a fighter's purse money after training expenses, 30 per cent for major championship contests.

No dispute is conceivable about Lawless's management credentials. Working from a gymnasium over the Royal Oak, a public house in Canning Town, Lawless is consistently involved at the highest levels of the game and four of his boxers, Charlie Magri (flyweight), Jim Watt (lightweight), John H. Stracey (welterweight), and Maurice Hope (light-middleweight), became world champions.

Long before Bruno turned professional, Lawless formed an alliance with Mickey Duff, Mike Barrett and Jarvis Astaire. Duff, born Monik Prager in a Polish ghetto, achieved little in the ring but has since acquired a reputation as a shrewd judge of fighters and a belligerently astute negotiator. He is a licensed manager, matchmaker and promoter and now operates mostly in the United States. Barrett, who later broke from the group, was Duff's partner. Astaire, an entrepreneur and deputy chairman of Wembley Stadium, is a discreet but significant force in the sport. They had exclusive boxing access to Wembley and the Royal Albert Hall and a lucrative contract with BBC television.

They did not possess a marketable heavyweight, but Bruno – tall, strong and impressively muscular – looked the part. The majority of black fighters find it difficult to overcome the prejudice that can still be detected in London boxing arenas. Lloyd Honeyghan brought off a notable victory in October 1986, defeating Donald Curry to become the undisputed welterweight champion, but when he defended his title against Jorge Vaca at the Grand Hall, Wembley, 12 months later, the promoters gave away hundreds of tickets to avoid the embarrassment of a half-empty hall.

Bruno fought for the first time as a professional at the Royal Albert Hall in London on 17 March 1982. The opponent, Lupe Guerra, had lost his five previous contests and was knocked out in the first round. Thirteen days later, Bruno appeared at Wembley against Harvey Steichen, who came with a record of five victories and five defeats. He was stopped in the second round. Tom Stevenson went down before the first round was completed when Bruno returned to the Albert Hall on 20 April.

Matchmaking has always been a contentious issue in boxing and some of the greatest champions, including Rocky Marciano, were fed easy opponents in the formative phase of their professional careers. The difficulty in making contests for inexperienced boxers was put perfectly by the American writer A. J. Liebling in his book *The Sweet Science*. 'In any art the prodigy presents a problem. Given too easy a problem, he goes slack, but asked too hard a question early, he becomes discouraged. The trick lies in keeping the fellow entertained while enriching his curriculum.'

Lawless and Duff were keeping Bruno entertained but it was soon abundantly clear that they were not dealing with a prodigy. The quick, with practice, can get quicker. The slow remain slow. Bruno is slow.

Bruno's first ten contests lasted a mere 17 rounds, his next four a total of 12 rounds. In order to suppress criticism, it was necessary to match him with a better class of opponent. Lawless and Duff chose Scott Le Doux, an experienced but ring-worn American who had been in with a number of leading heavyweights, including Larry Holmes, who knocked him out in the seventh round when defending the World Boxing Council championship in July 1980. The contest took place on 3 May 1983 at Wembley Arena. Le Doux was in poor shape and 20 lb above his best fighting weight. 'It was a pay day,' he said.

Frank Bruno after being overwhelmed by Mike Tyson at Las Vegas on 25 February 1989.

'If I won, fine. If I lost, what the hell? The money was reasonable and it meant that my wife, who was recovering from a cancer operation, could visit London and Paris.'

Le Doux was stopped in the third round and then retired from boxing, an utterly spent fighter.

Bruno had still to be asked serious questions. Neither his chin nor his stamina had been tested; the first crisis came on 11 October 1983 when he was matched with Floyd 'Jumbo' Cummings, another American, at the Albert Hall. Cummings had not won since June 1981. Towards the end of the first round he delivered a hopeful right swing that looped untidily into the left side of Bruno's head. Bruno was transfixed, his senses dishevelled, eyes vacant, legs twitching.

Jimmy Tibbs, then Bruno's trainer, was in the corner with Lawless. 'Had Frank attempted to take a step he would have gone over,' Tibbs said. 'Fortunately he was still upright at the bell and we were able to grab him. It could all have ended right there.' Cummings did not develop the advantage and Bruno, recovering steadily, stopped him in the seventh round. The crowd rose to Bruno, and his mentors were encouraged to broaden their horizon.

Five months earlier, Bruno knocked out Mike Jameson in Chicago. The contest was shown live by the BBC, but although readers of popular British tabloids were led to believe

USA

otherwise, viewing in the United States was restricted to a local station.

Shamelessly subjective reporting of Bruno's contests evoked a scathing condemnation in the satirical magazine *Private Eye*, beneath the headline 'Blim, Duff and Lawless'. 'The massed ranks of Fleet Street's boxing hacks and those never wallet-weary executives of BBC TV are readying the superlatives to celebrate another forward step by Britain's Great Black hope, heavyweight Frank Bruno. As the *Eye* went to press, Bruno was due in the Wembley ring to face yet one more American import designed to beef up his reputation as a potential world beater, a reputation somewhat dented by the aptly named "Bone-crusher" Smith.'

Bruno's advisers were on the defensive before Smith knocked him out in the tenth round at Wembley on 13 May 1984. In December 1983, the *Sunday Mirror* published a withering assessment by Larry Holmes, the heavyweight champion who had sparred a couple of rounds with Bruno. 'I know how much the British public want him to be a champion,' Holmes wrote. 'But he isn't good enough. Mickey Duff will build him a record and get him a title shot, but my belief is that he will get knocked out.'

Two days after the article appeared, Jarvis Astaire indicated his disappointment to Robert Edwards, then editor of the *Sunday Mirror*, following a Variety Club lunch at the Savoy Hotel. Three weeks later, Duff sought out Holmes at the World Boxing Council annual convention in Las Vegas. He produced a clipping from the *Sunday Mirror* that Holmes recognized as an interview he had given to Ed Schuyler of the Associated Press agency. Holmes thought it to be a bland version of the original. Duff tried again. 'Do you know they paid twenty-five thousand dollars for this?' he said. (Schuyler did not ask for a fee.) 'The man is my friend,' replied Holmes. 'I wish they had paid him fifty thousand dollars.'

In an attempt to give Bruno credibility in the United States, an agreement was reached with NBC, the American television network which employs Dr Ferdie Pacheco as a boxing analyst. Pacheco, who administered for many years to Muhammad Ali, is friendly with Astaire.

The least threatening of four opponents suggested by NBC was James 'Bonecrusher' Smith. A college graduate, a former army sergeant and prison guard, he had been boxing for only two years and was not ranked in the top 20 American heavyweights. Smith was astonished by the attention he received in London. 'I'd never known anything like it,' he said. 'It was frightening.'

For ten rounds it looked as though Bruno would surmount the hurdle. Then Smith connected with his right and Bruno went down from a volley of blows.

210

The defeat so devastated Lawless that he thought seriously about retiring from boxing. Bruno was less discouraged. He persuaded Lawless to attend a Press conference the following day and was soon back in the gymnasium.

Tibbs, who later parted from Lawless, once again set about trying to eliminate the flaws. 'Frank is very determined and willing, and he works hard at anything he's shown,' he said. 'But there is no natural ability. He's very strong but stiffens up in the ring and relies too much on his jab. Mobile opponents confuse him. And there is no instinct for holding and hanging on when he gets hurt. I wanted Lawless to bring in some tough sparring partners but he wasn't keen. You can over-protect fighters.'

On 1 October 1985, Bruno knocked out Anders Eklund of Sweden to win the European championship. As a result, he was automatically ranked in the world top ten. On 4 March 1986 he met Gerrie Coetzee, a white South African who had been the World Boxing Association champion. Coetzee was approaching the end of his career but the contest was sanctioned as an official eliminator for the WBA title held by Tim Witherspoon. Coetzee had grown fat and Bruno got rid of him in the first round at Wembley.

As the result of Fleet Street hyperbole, Bruno arrived in his corner an odds-on favourite to take the championship from Witherspoon at Wembley on 19 July 1986. Visitors to the champion's training camp at Basildon in Essex were astonished by his lethargic routines. He had admitted to drug abuse and was in conflict with Don King, the American promoter whose son, Carl, managed him. Bruno held his own for ten rounds but the eleventh proved disastrous. Witherspoon landed a right and Bruno fell backwards, worryingly slack jawed, his inability to withstand a crisis evident again. Witherspoon completed the devastation and the contest was stopped.

After stopping James Tillis in March 1987, Bruno fought Chuck Gardner, a pathetically inadequate American rejected as an opponent by the Board of Control two years earlier; they had no jurisdiction over a contest that took place in Cannes. 'Nevertheless we should have expressed our concern more vigorously,' admitted John Morris, the Board's general secretary.

The embarrassment of a first round knock-out, transmitted live by BBC television, finally persuaded Mike Barrett to end his association with Lawless, Duff and Astaire. 'It was ludicrous,' he said. 'The public were not getting value for money.'

On 24 October 1987, Bruno defeated Joe Bugner at White Hart Lane, the Tottenham Hotspur football ground. Bugner, the

211

Hungarian-born former British and European heavyweight champion, twice retired, under-trained and by then an Australian citizen, offered only token resistance and was stopped in the eighth round.

At the World Boxing Council annual convention in London six days later, Bruno was made the number one contender for Mike Tyson's championship. He has not been risked since.

* * * * *

By the time Mike Tyson and Frank Bruno came together at the Las Vegas Hilton on 25 February 1989, Don King, the flamboyant American promoter and former numbers racketeer from Cleveland, had become a loud and persuasive force in the champion's life, seizing an opportunity to regain control of the heavyweight division, employing his unique brand of oratory to persuade all inhabitants of the universe that he and Tyson were an unbeatable team.

This further complicated matters, but to watch Tyson train at Johnny Tocco's gymnasium, an entirely functional establishment set in a section of Las Vegas that could be downtown anywhere, was to be reacquainted with the impression that few men have gone to the ring possessing such natural powers of devastation.

Bruno was encouraged by suggestions that Tyson might have left some of his strength and speed in bars and discotheques but as the champion had three weeks in which to sharpen up, his trainers were not alarmed by fractional errors of judgement. Tyson looked well and according to his friend Jay Bright, a 30-year-old New Yorker who had been appointed to supervise training following the split with Kevin Rooney, had set aside the psychological problems that appeared to be threatening his career.

When sitting on a bench in the middle of the ring, while interrogators crowded into a narrow passage left between the ropes and a wall of the gymnasium, Tyson looked relaxed and the responses came easily. He admitted to outbreaks of wild behaviour and bleak periods of depression. 'All that's over with,' he insisted. 'I'm back where I belong.'

The tourists, the three-day guests, the ones with planes to catch and losses to account for, mostly middle-aged and predominantly oriental, were soon visibly perplexed by the arrival in Las Vegas of brash British patriots who conveyed the impression that they were in urgent need of psychiatric attention.

This related most profoundly to their unbridled enthusiasm for an event that in American terms was little more than an opportunity to discover the state of Tyson's mind. It was assumed, and without debate, that Bruno would fall, but when and in which direction? In that respect there was no better witness in town than Michael Spinks, who was foolishly thought to have been capable of confusing and beating Tyson when they had met in Atlantic City six months earlier.

Spinks, who retired after the contest (he received a purse of more than £5 million), remembered the experience vividly. 'Nothing surprises me about Tyson,' he said. 'He punches with tremendous force and hits you everywhere. When he hits you in the arms, it paralyses them. Before I fought him, people kept asking me about a plan. I let them think we had worked out something, but it's impossible to do this. I went in there hoping there might be a way, that he would make a mistake. You've got to land your punch before he lands his.'

When Spinks said Bruno had as good a chance as any other heavyweight, it was another way of saying that Tyson is unbeatable. 'I don't know much about Bruno,' he added. 'I hear he hits pretty good, but unless he can outmanoeuvre Tyson, he can forget it.'

Bruno's cohorts apart, this was a substantially popular point of view and in the betting emporiums they laid even money that the challenger would not survive for longer than four rounds.

★ ★ ★ ★ ★

Bruno was stopped after 2 minutes 55 seconds of the fifth round but when the bell sounded to end the fourth a roar went up from those who had invested in him to get that far. The British heavyweight never came close to even sharing any of the completed rounds but recovered from an early knock-down to frustrate the champion, staggering him with a left hook.

In the light of subsequent dramatic events a more accomplished challenger might have taken sensational advantage of Tyson's mental state. Certainly some doubts were raised at ringside when the champion persisted in trying to tear Bruno apart with wild hooks, seldom employing his stiff jab to set up openings, driving in with his head and elbows as though the technical disciplines painstakingly imposed by D'Amato and Kevin Rooney had been abandoned to frustration and rage. And as Tyson's handlers looked bewildered and nervous, completely in awe of their man, it was easily concluded that the break with Rooney might prove disastrous.

Tyson answered this in brutal fashion, knocking out Carl 'The' Truth Williams in one round, but then withdrew controversially from a defence against Donovan 'Razor' Ruddock in Edmonton, Canada, claiming that an illness had interrupted his preparation.

Despite suspicions that he could no longer be relied upon to show up regularly in the gymnasium, Tyson was not thought to be in any peril when agreeing to put up the championship against James 'Buster' Douglas, a 29 year-old from Columbus, Ohio who had no sporting distinction beyond sharing a birthplace with Jack Nicklaus.

Nothing in Douglas's record suggested better than a moderate scuffler and in gathering it he had occasionally given the impression that an offer of alternative employment would be given serious consideration.

He had been stopped by David Bey, Tony Tucker and Mike White but it was a miserable draw against Steffan Tangstadt, an inept Norwegian, that prompted his father, a former professional middleweight, to leave the ringside in despair.

Taking all this into account I decided against travelling to Tokyo in February 1990, believing Douglas would not last more than a couple of rounds, although experiencing a tremor of doubt when Tyson was floored by a sparring partner. A familiar promotional ploy or fresh evidence that Tyson was finding it increasingly difficult to maintain an aura of invincibility. Did Douglas indeed have a chance? These were suddenly good questions but confidence was quickly restored when Las Vegas casinos suspended betting on the contest.

In fact Douglas appeared to be so much of an underdog that only a handful of American boxing writers crossed the Pacific. Then shock in sport took on a new dimension.

Even at long range it soon became clear that Douglas was the least intimidated of Tyson's championship opponents, as though a series of domestic traumas, his mother's death a week before leaving for Tokyo, a terminal illness endured by the mother of his 11 year-old son, and a broken marriage, had given him a new perspective about the hardships of boxing.

It was also clear that the Mike Tyson who brought terror to the heavyweight division had not shown up in Japan. Instead of taut menace his heavily muscled body conveyed an unavoidable impression of softness and as the contest developed an air of resignation settled on normally truculent features.

Nevertheless people who had not seen a lot of Douglas found it difficult to believe what they were seeing when he set about Tyson as though convinced that the heavyweight champion was more myth than pulverizing reality.

The chastising left jabs and powerful following rights Douglas employed when introducing Tyson to a new and shattering experience in the professional ring were delivered with such confidence and authority that it became appropriate to think of him not only as a born-again Christian but a born-again fighter.

Cumulatively effective those blows wore Tyson down and his reputation was further undermined by Don King's monstrous attempt

214

to persuade the notoriously pliable officials of the World Boxing Association and the World Boxing Council that a re-match was in order. This was based on the utterly spurious contention that an imprecise count had enabled Douglas to avoid a knockout in the 8th round thus invalidating the sensational victory he achieved with a pulverizing assault in the tenth.

Coming under heavy fire from across the world King was forced to acknowledge Douglas as the undisputed champion but held him to a promotional contract, an arrangement that led to complex legal activity first in Nevada then New Jersey.

By June 1990, almost four months after recording the biggest upset in boxing this century Douglas was still waiting for an opportunity to prove it had not been a fluke while Tyson began his rehabilitation against Henry Tillman who twice beat him as an amateur.

 215

RECORDS

ROCKY MARCIANO

(The Brockton Blockbuster)
Born, September 1, 1923, Brockton, Mass.
Weight, 184 lbs Height, 5 ft. 10¼ in. Managed by AL Weill.

1947			
Mar. 17	Lee Epperson, Holyoke, Mass	KO	3
1948			
July 12	Harry Bilazarian, Providence	KO	1
July 19	John Edwards, Providence	KO	1
Aug. 9	Bobby Quinn, Providence	KO	3
Aug. 23	Eddie Ross, Providence	KO	1
Aug. 30	Jimmy Weeks, Providence	KO	1
Sept. 13	Jerry Jackson, Providence	KO	1
Sept. 20	Bill Hardeman, Providence	KO	1
Sept. 30	Gil Cardione, Washington, D.C.	KO	1
Oct. 4	Bob Jefferson, Providence	KO	2
Nov. 29	Pat Connolly, Providence	KO	1
Dec. 14	Gilley Ferron, Philadelphia	KO	2
1949			
Mar. 21	Johnny Pretzie, Providence	KO	5
Mar. 28	Artie Donato, Providence	KO	1
Apr. 11	James Walls, Providence	KO	3
May 2	Jimmy Evans, Providence	KO	3
May 23	Don Mogard, Providence	W	10
July 18	Harry Haft, Providence	KO	3
Aug.16	Pete Louthis, New Bedford	KO	3
Sept. 26	Tommy DiGiogio, Providence	KO	4
Oct. 10	Ted Lowry, Providence	W	10
Nov. 7	Joe Dominic, Providence	KO	2
Dec. 2	Pat Richards, New York	KO	2
Dec. 19	Phil Muscato, Providence	KO	5
Dec. 30	Carmine Vingo, New York	KO	6
1950			
Mar. 24	Roland LaStarza, New York	W	10
June 5	Eldridge Eatman, Providence	KO	3
July 10	Gino Buonvino, Boston	KO	10
Sept. 18	Johnny Shkor, Providence	KO	6
Nov. 13	Ted Lowry, Providence	W	10
Dec. 18	Bill Wilson, Providence	KO	1
1951			
Jan. 29	Keene Simmons, Providence	KO	8
Mar. 20	Harold Mitchell, Hartford	KO	2
Mar. 26	Art Henri, Providence	KO	9
Apr. 30	Red Applegate, Providence	W	10
July 12	Red Layne, New York	KO	6
Aug. 27	Freddie Beshore, Boston	KO	4
Oct. 26	Joe Louis, New York	KO	8
1952			
Feb. 13	Lee Savold, Philadelphia	KO	6
Apr. 21	Gino Buonvino, Providence	KO	2
May 12	Bernie Reynolds, Providence	KO	3
July 28	Harry (Kid) Matthews, New York	KO	2
Sept. 23	Jersey Joe Walcott, Philadelphia (Won World Heavyweight Title)	KO	13
1953			
May 15	Jersey Joe Walcott, Chicago (Retained World Heavyweight Title)	KO	1
Sept. 24	Roland LaStarza, New York (Retained World Heavyweight Title)	KO	11
1954			
June 17	Ezzard Charles, New York (Retained World Heavyweight Title)	W	15
Sept. 17	Ezzard Charles, New York (Retained World Heavyweight Title)	KO	8
1955			
May 16	Don Cockell, San Francisco (Retained World Heavyweight Title)	KO	9
Sept. 21	Archie Moore, New York (Retained World Heavyweight Title)	KO	9
1956			
Apr. 27	Announced retirement		

TB	KO	WD	WF	D	LD	LF	KO BY	ND	NC
49	43	6	0	0	0	0	0	0	0

Elected to Boxing Hall of Fame, 1959.
Died, August 31, 1969, in an airplane accident in Newton, Iowa.

SUGAR RAY ROBINSON

(Walker Smith, Jr.)
Born, May 3, 1921, Detroit, Mich. Weight,
145–157 lbs. Height, 5ft 11½ in. Managed by George Gainford.

1940			
Oct. 4	Joe Escheverria, New York	KO	2
Oct. 8	Silent Stefford, Savannah	KO	2
Oct. 22	Mistos Grispos, New York	W	6
Nov. 11	Bobby Woods, Philadelphia	KO	1
Dec. 9	Norment Quarles, Philadelphia	KO	4
Dec. 12	Oliver White, New York	KO	3
1941			
Jan. 4	Henry LaBarba, Brooklyn	KO	1
Jan. 13	Frankie Wallace, Philadelphia	KO	1
Jan. 31	George Zengaras, New York	W	6
Feb. 8	Benny Cartegena, Brooklyn	KO	1
Feb. 21	Bobby McIntire, New York	W	6
Feb. 27	Gene Spencer, Detroit	KO	5
Mar. 3	Jimmy Tygh, Philadelphia	KO	8
Apr. 14	Jimmy Tygh, Philadelphia	KO	1
Apr. 24	Charley Burns, Atlantic City	KO	1
Apr. 30	Joe Ghnouly, Washington, D.C.	KO	3
May 10	Vic Troise, Brooklyn	KO	1
May 19	Nick Castiglione, Philadelphia	KO	1
June 16	Mike Evans, Philadelphia	KO	2
July 2	Pete Lello, New York	KO	4
July 21	Sammy Angott, Philadelphia	W	10

Rocky Marciano and Don Cockell, May 1955

Date	Opponent	Result	Rounds
Aug. 27	Carl (Red) Guggino, Long Island City	KO	3
Aug. 29	Maurice Arnault, Atlantic City	KO	1
Sept. 19	Maxie Shapiro, New York	KO	3
Sept. 25	Marty Servo, Philadelphia	W	10
Oct. 31	Fritzie Zivic, New York	W	10
1942			
Jan. 16	Fritzie Zivic, New York	KO	10
Feb. 20	Maxie Berger, New York	KO	2
Mar. 20	Norman Rubio, New York	KO	7
Apr. 17	Harvey Dubs, Detroit	KO	6
Apr. 30	Dick Banner, Minneapolis	KO	2
May 28	Marty Servo, New York	W	10
July 31	Sammy Angott, New York	W	10
Aug. 21	Ruben Shank, New York	KO	2
Aug. 27	Tony Motisi, Chicago	KO	1
Oct. 2	Jake LaMotta, New York	W	10
Oct. 19	Izzy Jannazzo, Philadelphia	W	10
Nov. 6	Vic Dellicurti, New York	W	10
Dec. 1	Izzy Jannazzo, Cleveland	KO	8
Dec. 14	Al Nettlow, Philadelphia	KO	3
1943			
Feb. 5	Jack LaMotta, Detroit	L	10
Feb. 19	Jackie Wilson, New York	W	10
Feb. 26	Jake LaMotta, Detroit	W	10
Apr. 30	Freddie Cabral, Boston	KO	1
July 1	Ralph Zannelli, Boston	W	10
Aug. 27	Henry Armstrong, New York	W	10
1944			
Oct. 13	Izzy Jannazzo, Boston	KO	2
Oct. 27	Sgt. Lou Woods, Chicago	KO	9
Nov. 17	Vic Dellicurti, Detroit	W	10
Dec. 12	Sheik Rangel, Philadelphia	KO	2
Dec. 22	Georgie Martin, Boston	KO	7
1945			
Jan. 10	Billy Furrone, Washington, D.C.	KO	2
Jan. 16	Tommy Bell, Cleveland	W	10
Feb. 14	George Costner, Chicago	KO	1
Feb. 24	Jake LaMotta, New York	W	10
May 14	Jose Basora, Philadelphia	D	10
June 15	Jimmy McDaniels, New York	KO	2
Sept. 18	Jimmy Mandell, Buffalo	KO	5
Sept. 26	Jake LaMotta, Chicago	W	12
Dec. 4	Vic Dellicurti, Boston	W	10
1946			
Jan. 14	Dave Clark, Pittsburgh	KO	2
Feb. 5	Tony Riccio, Elizabeth	KO	4
Feb. 15	O'Neill Bell, Detroit	KO	2
Feb. 26	Cliff Beckett, St Louis	KO	4
Mar. 4	Sammy Angott, Pittsburgh	W	10
Mar. 14	Izzy Jannazzo, Baltimore	W	10
Mar. 21	Freddy Flores, New York	KO	5
June 12	Freddy Wilson, Worcester	KO	2
June 25	Norman Rubio, Union City	W	10
July 12	Joe Curcio, New York	KO	2
Aug. 15	Vinnie Vines, Albany	KO	6
Sept. 25	Sidney Miller, Elizabeth	KO	3
Oct. 7	Ossie Harris, Pittsburgh	W	10
Nov. 1	Cecil Hudson, Detroit	KO	6
Nov. 6	Artie Levine, Cleveland	KO	10
Dec. 20	Tommy Bell, New York (Won Vacant World Welterweight Title)	W	15
1947			
Mar. 27	Bernie Miller, Miami	KO	3
Apr. 3	Fred Wilson, Akron	KO	3
Apr. 8	Eddie Finazzo, Kansas City	KO	4
May 16	Georgie Abrams, New York	W	10
June 24	Jimmy Doyle, Cleveland (Retained World Welterweight Title)	KO	8
Aug. 21	Sammy Secreet, Akron	KO	1
Aug. 29	Flashy Sebastian, New York	KO	1
Oct. 28	Jackie Wilson, Los Angeles	KO	7
Dec. 10	Billy Nixon, Elizabeth	KO	6
Dec. 19	Chuck Taylor, Detroit (Retained World Welterweight Title)	KO	6
1948			
Mar. 4	Ossie Harris, Toledo	W	10
Mar. 16	Henry Brimm, Buffalo	W	10
June 28	Bernard Docusen, Chicago (Retained World Welterweight Title)	W	15
Sept. 23	Kid Gavilan, New York	W	10
Nov. 15	Bobby Lee, Philadelphia	W	10
1949			
Feb. 10	Gene Buffalo, Wilkes-Barre	KO	1
Feb. 15	Henry Brimm, Buffalo	D	10
Mar. 25	Bobby Lee, Chicago	W	10
Apr. 11	Don Lee, Omaha	W	10
Apr. 20	Earl Turner, Oakland	KO	8
May 16	Al Tribuani, Wilmington	Exh.	4
June 7	Freddie Flores, New Bedford	KO	3
June 20	Cecil Hudson, Providence	KO	5
July 11	Kid Gavilan, Philadelphia (Retained World Welterweight Title)	W	15
Aug. 24	Steve Belloise, New York	KO	7
Sept. 2	Al Mobley, Chicago	Exh	4
Sept. 9	Benny Evans, Omaha	KO	5
Sept 12	Charley Dotson, Houston	KO	3
Nov. 9	Don Lee, Denver	W	10
Nov. 13	Vern Lester, New Orleans	KO	5
Nov. 15	Gene Burton, Shreveport	Exh.	6
Nov. 16	Gene Burton, Dallas	Exh.	6
1950			
Jan. 30	George LaRover, New Haven	KO	4
Feb. 13	Al Mobley, Miami	KO	6
Feb. 22	Aaron Wade, Savannah	KO	3
Feb. 27	Jean Walzack, St. Louis	W	10
Mar. 22	George Costner, Philadelphia	KO	1
Apr. 21	Cliff Beckett, Columbus	KO	3
Apr. 28	Ray Barnes, Detroit	W	10
June 5	Robert Villemain, Philadelphia (Won Vacant Pennsylvania World Middleweight Title)	W	15
Aug. 9	Charley Fusari, Jersey City (Retained World Welterweight Title)	W	15
Aug. 25	Jose Basora, Scranton (Retained Pennsylvania World Middleweight Title)	KO	1

Sugar Ray Robinson and Terry Downes, September 1962

Date	Opponent	Result	Rounds
Sept. 4	Billy Brown, New York	W	10
Oct. 16	Joe Rindone, Boston	KO	6
Oct. 26	Carl (Bobo) Olson, Philadelphia (Retained Pennsylvania World Middleweight Title)	KO	12
Nov. 8	Bobby Dykes, Chicago	W	10
Nov. 27	Jean Stock, Paris	KO	2
Dec. 9	Luc Van Dam, Brussels	KO	4
Dec. 16	Jean Walzack, Geneva	W	10
Dec. 22	Robert Villemain, Paris	KO	9
Dec. 25	Hans Stretz, Frankfort	KO	5
1951			
Feb. 14	Jake LaMotta, Chicago (Won World Middleweight Title)	KO	13
Apr. 5	Holley Mims, Miami	W	10
Apr. 9	Don Ellis, Oklahoma City	KO	1
May 21	Kid Marcel, Paris	KO	5
May 26	Jean Wanes, Zurich	W	10
June 10	Jan de Bruin, Antwerp	KO	8
June 16	Jean Walzack, Liege	KO	6
June 24	Gerhard Hecht, Berlin	NC	2
July 1	Cyrille Delannoit, Turin	KO	3
July 10	Randy Turpin, London (Lost World Middleweight Title)	L	15
Sept. 12	Randy Turpin, New York (Regained World Middleweight Title)	KO	10
1952			
Mar. 13	Carl (Bobo) Olson, San Francisco (Retained World Middleweight Title)	W	15
Apr. 16	Rocky Graziano, Chicago (Retained World Middleweight Title)	KO	3
June 25	Joey Maxim, New York	KO by	14
Dec. 18	Announced retirement.		
1953	(Inactive)		
1954			
Oct. 20	Announced return to ring		
Nov. 29	Gene Burton, Hamilton	Exh.	6
1955			
Jan. 5	Joe Rindone, Detroit	KO	6
Jan. 19	Ralph (Tiger) Jones, Chicago	L	10
Mar. 29	Johnny Lombardo, Cincinnati	W	10
Apr. 14	Ted Olla, Milwaukee	KO	3
May 4	Garth Panter, Detroit	W	10
July 22	Rocky Castellani, San Francisco	W	10
Dec. 9	Carl (Bobo) Olson, Chicago (Regained World Middleweight Title)	KO	2
1956			
May 18	Carl (Bobo) Olson, Los Angeles (Retained World Middleweight Title)	KO	4
Nov. 10	Bob Provizzi, New Haven	W	10
1957			
Jan. 2	Gene Fullmer, New York (Lost World Middleweight Title)	L	15
May. 1	Gene Fullmer, Chicago (Regained World Middleweight Title)	KO	5
Sept. 10	Otis Woodard, Philadelphia	Exh.	2
Sept. 10	Lee Williams, Philadelphia	Esh.	2
Sept. 23	Carmen Basilio, New York (Lost World Middleweight Title)	L	15
1958			
Mar. 25	Carmen Basilio, Chicago (Regained World Middleweight Title)	W	15
1959			
Dec. 14	Bob Young, Boston	KO	2
1960			
Jan. 22	Paul Pender, Boston (Lost World Middleweight Title)	L	15
Apr. 2	Tony Baldoni, Baltimore	KO	1
June 10	Paul Pender, Boston (For World Middleweight Title)	L	15
Dec. 3	Gene Fullmer, Los Angeles (For NBA Middleweight Title)	D	15
1961			
Mar. 4	Gene Fullmer, Las Vegas (For NBA Middleweight Title)	L	15
Sept. 25	Wilf Greaves, Detroit	W	10
Oct. 21	Denny Moyer, New York	W	10
Nov. 20	Al Hauser, Providence	KO	6
Dec. 8	Wilf Greaves, Pittsburgh	KO	8
1962			
Feb. 17	Denny Moyer, New York	L	10
Apr. 27	Bobby Lee, Port of Spain	KO	2
July 9	Phil Moyer, Los Angeles	L	10
Sept. 25	Terry Downes, London	L	10
Oct. 17	Diego Infantes, Vienna	KO	2
Nov. 10	Georges Estatoff, Lyons	KO	6
1963			
Jan. 30	Ralph Dupas, Miami Beach	W	10
Feb. 25	Bernie Reynolds, Santo Domingo	KO	4
Mar. 11	Billy Thornton, Lewiston	KO	3
May 5	Maurice Rolbnet, Sherbrooke	KO	3
June 24	Joey Giardello, Philadelphia	L	10
Oct. 14	Armand Vanucci, Paris	W	10
Nov. 9	Fabio Bettini, Lyons	D	10
Nov. 16	Emile Sarens, Brussels	KO	8
Nov. 29	Andre Davier, Grenoble	W	10
Dec. 9	Armand Vanucci, Paris	W	10
1964			
May 19	Gaylord Barnes, Portland	W	10
July 8	Clarence Riley, Pittsfield	KO	6
July 27	Art Hernandez, Omaha	D	10
Sept. 3	Mick Leahy, Paisley	L	10
Sept. 28	Yolande Leveque, Paris	W	10
Oct. 12	Johnny Angel, London	KO	6
Oct. 24	Jackie Caillau, Nice	W	10
Nov. 7	Baptiste Rolland, Calen	W	10
Nov. 14	Jean Beltritti, Marseilles	W	10
Nov. 27	Fabio Bettini, Rome	D	10
1965			
Mar. 6	Jimmy Beecham, Kingston	KO	2
Apr. 4	East Basting, Savannah	KO	1
Apr. 28	Rocky Randall, Norfolk	KO	3

Joe Frazier and Muhammad Ali, March 1971

May 5	Rocky Randall, Jacksonville	W	8
May 24	Memo Ayon, Tijuana	L	10
June 1	Stan Harrington, Honolulu	L	10
June 24	Young Joe Walcott, Richmond	W	10
July 12	Ferd Hernandez, Las Vegas	L	10
July 27	Young Joe Walcott, Richmond	W	10
Aug. 10	Stan Harrington, Honolulu	L	10
Sept. 15	Neil Morrison, Norfolk	NC	2
Sept. 23	Young Joe Walcott, Philadelphia	W	10
Oct. 1	Peter Schmidt, Johnstown	W	10
Oct. 20	Rudolph Bent, Steubenville	KO	3
Nov. 10	Joey Archer, Pittsburgh	L	10
Dec. 10	Announced retirement		

TB	KO	WD	WF	D	LD	LF	KO BY	ND	NC
201	109	65	0	6	18	0	1	0	2

Elected to Boxing Hall of Fame, 1967.

JOE FRAZIER

(Smokin' Joe)
Born, January 12, 1944, Beaufort, S.C. Weight, 205 lbs. Height, 5 ft. 11½ in.
1964 Olympic Heavyweight Gold Medalist

1965			
Aug. 16	Woody Goss, Philadelphia	KO	1
Sept. 20	Mike Bruce, Philadelphia	KO	3
Sept. 28	Ray Staples, Philadelphia	KO	2
Nov. 11	Abe Davis, Philadelphia	KO	1
1966			
Jan. 17	Mel Turnbow, Philadelphia	KO	1
Mar. 4	Dick Wipperman, New York	KO	5
Apr. 4	Charley Polite, Philadelphia	KO	2
Apr. 28	Don (Toro) Smith, Pittsburgh	KO	3
May 19	Chuck Leslie, Los Angeles	KO	3
May 26	Memphis Al Jones, Los Angeles	KO	1
July 25	Billy Daniels, Philadelphia	KO	6
Sept. 21	Oscar Bonavena, New York	W	10
Nov. 21	Eddie Machen, Los Angeles	KO	10
1967			
Feb. 21	Doug Jones, Philadelphia	KO	6
Apr. 11	Jeff Davis, Miami Beach	KO	5
May 4	George Johnson, Los Angeles	W	10
July 19	George Chuvalo, New York	KO	4
Oct. 17	Tony Doyle, Philadelphia	KO	2
Dec. 18	Marion Connors, Boston	KO	3
1968			
Mar. 4	Buster Mathis, New York (Won Vacant New York World Heavyweight Title)	KO	11
June 24	Manuel Ramos, New York (Retained New York World Heavyweight Title)	KO	2
Dec. 10	Oscar Bonavena, Philadelphia (Retained New York World Heavyweight Title)	W	15
1969			
Apr. 22	Dave Zyglewicz, Houston (Retained New York World Heavyweight Title)	KO	1
June 23	Jerry Quarry, New York (Retained New York World Heavyweight Title)	KO	7
1970			
Feb. 16	Jimmy Ellis, New York (Won Vacant World Heavyweight Title)	KO	5
Nov. 18	Bob Foster, Detroit (Retained World Heavyweight Title)	KO	2
1971			
Mar. 8	Muhammad Ali, New York (Retained World Heavyweight Title)	W	15
July 15	Cleveland Williams, Houston	Exh.	3
July 15	James Helwig, Houston	Exh.	3
1972			
Jan. 15	Terry Daniels, New Orleans (Retained World Heavyweight Title)	KO	4
May 25	Ron Stander, Omaha (Retained World Heavyweight Title)	KO	5
1973			
Jan. 22	George Foreman, Kingston (Lost World Heavyweight Title)	KO by	2
July 2	Joe Bugner, London	W	12
1974			
Jan. 28	Muhammad Ali, New York (For NABF Heavyweight Title)	L	12
June 17	Jerry Quarry, New York	KO	5
1975			
Mar. 1	Jimmy Ellis, Melbourne	KO	9
Oct. 1	Muhammad Ali, Manila (For World Heavyweight Title)	KO by	14
1976			
June 15	George Foreman, Uniondale	KO by	5
1977–1980	(Inactive)		
1981			
Dec. 3	Jumbo Cummings, Chicago	D	10

TB	KO	WD	WF	D	LD	LF	KO BY	ND	NC
37	27	5	0	1	1	0	3	0	0

Elected to Boxing Hall of Fame, 1980.

Pensive Muhammad Ali

MUHAMMAD ALI

(Cassius Marcellus Clay, Jr.)
(The Louisville Lip)
Born, January 17, 1942, Louisville, Ky. Weight, 186–230 lbs. Height, 6 ft. 3 in.
1959 National AAU Light Heavyweight Champion
1960 National AAU Light Heavyweight Champion
1960 Olympic Light Heavyweight Gold Medalist

Date	Opponent	Result	Rounds
1960			
Oct. 29	Tunney Hunsaker, Louisville	W	6
Dec. 27	Herb Siler, Miami Beach	KO	4
1961			
Jan. 17	Tony Esperti, Miami Beach	KO	3
Feb. 7	Jim Robinson, Miami Beach	KO	1
Feb. 21	Donnie Fleeman, Miami Beach	KO	7
Apr. 19	Lamar Clark, Louisville	KO	2
June 26	Duke Sabedong, Las Vegas	W	10
July 22	Alonzo Johnson, Louisville	W	10
Oct. 7	Alex Miteff, Louisville	KO	6
Nov. 29	Willi Besmanoff, Louisville	KO	7
1962			
Feb. 10	Sonny Banks, New York	KO	4
Feb. 28	Don Warner, Miami Beach	KO	4
Apr. 23	George Logan, Los Angeles	KO	4
May 19	Billy Daniels, New York	KO	7
July 20	Alejandro Lavorante, Los Angeles	KO	5
Nov. 15	Archie Moore, Los Angeles	KO	4
1963			
Jan. 24	Charlie Powell, Pittsburgh	KO	3
Mar. 13	Doug Jones, New York	W	10
June 18	Henry Cooper, London	KO	5
1964			
Feb. 25	Sonny Liston, Miami Beach (Won World Heavyweight Title)	KO	7
1965			
May 25	Sonny Liston, Lewiston, Me (Retained World Heavyweight Title)	KO	1
July 31	Jimmy Ellis, San Juan, P.R.	Exh.	3
July 31	Cody Jones, San Juan, P.R.	Exh.	3
Aug. 16	Cody Jones, Gothenburg	Exh.	2
Aug. 16	Jimmy Ellis, Gothenburg	Exh.	2
Aug. 20	Jimmy Ellis, London, England	Exh.	4
Aug. 20	Cody Jones, Paisley, Scotland	Exh.	4
Nov. 22	Floyd Patterson, Las Vegas (Retained World Heavyweight Title)	KO	12
1966			
Mar. 29	George Chuvalo, Toronto (Retained World Heavyweight Title)	W	15
May 21	Henry Cooper, London, England (Retained World Heavyweight Title)	KO	6
Aug. 6	Brian London, London, England (Retained World Heavyweight Title)	KO	3
Sept. 10	Karl Mildenberger, Frankfurt (Retained World Heavyweight Title)	KO	12
Nov. 14	Cleveland Williams, Houston (Retained World Heavyweight Title)	KO	3
1967			
Feb. 6	Ernest Terrell, Houston (Retained World Heavyweight Title)	W	15
Mar. 22	Zora Folley, New York (Retained World Heavyweight Title)	KO	7
June 15	Alvin (Blue) Lewis, Detroit	Exh.	3
June 15	Orvill Qualls, Detroit	Exh.	3
1968–1969			
(Inactive)			
1970			
Feb. 3	Announced retirement		
Oct. 26	Jerry Quarry, Atlanta	KO	3
Dec. 7	Oscar Bonavena, New York	KO	15
1971			
Mar. 8	Joe Frazier, New York (For World Heavyweight Title)	L	15
June 25	J.D. McCauley, Dayton	Exh.	2
June 25	Eddie Brooks, Dayton	Exh.	3
June 25	Rufus Brassell, Dayton	Exh.	3
June 30	Alex Mack, Charleston	Exh.	3
June 30	Eddie Brooks, Charleston	Exh.	4
July 26	Jimmy Ellis, Houston (Won Vacant NABF Heavyweight Title)	KO	12
Aug. 21	Lancer Johnson, Caracas	Exh.	4
Aug. 21	Eddie Brooks, Caracas	Exh.	4
Aug. 23	Lancer Johnson, Port of Spain	Exh.	4
Aug. 23	Eddie Brooks, Port of Spain	Exh.	2
Nov. 6	James Summerville, Buenos Aires	Exh.	5
Nov. 6	Miguel Angel Paez, Buenos Aires	Exh.	5
Nov. 17	Buster Mathis, Houston, (Retained NABF Heavyweight Title)	W	12
Dec. 26	Jurgen Blin, Zurich, Switzerland	KO	7
1972			
Apr. 1	Mac Foster, Tokyo, Japan	W	15
May 1	George Chuvalo, Vancouver, B.C. (Retained NABF Heavyweight Title)	W	12
June 27	Jerry Quarry, Las Vegas (Retained NABF Heavyweight Title)	KO	7
July 1	Lonnie Bennett, Los Angeles	Exh.	2
July 1	Eddie Jones, Los Angeles	Exh.	2
July 1	Billy Ryan, Los Angeles	Exh.	2
July 1	Charley James, Los Angeles	Exh.	2
July 1	Rahaman Ali, Los Angeles	Exh.	2
July 19	Alvin (Blue) Lewis, Dublin	KO	11
Aug. 24	Obie English, Baltimore	Exh.	4
Aug. 24	Ray Anderson, Baltimore	Exh.	2
Aug. 24	Alonzo Johnson, Baltimore	Exh.	2
Aug. 24	George Hill, Baltimore	Exh.	2
Aug. 28	Alonzo Johnson, Cleveland	Exh.	2
Aug. 28	Amos Johnson, Cleveland	Exh.	2
Sept. 20	Floyd Patterson, New York (Retained NABF Heavyweight Title)	KO	7
Oct. 11	John (Dino) Denis, Boston	Exh.	2

Oct. 11	Cliff McDonald, Boston	Exh.	2
Oct. 11	Doug Kirk, Boston	Exh.	2
Oct. 11	Ray Anderson, Boston	Exh.	2
Oct. 21	Paul Raymond, Boston	Exh.	2
Nov. 21	Bob Foster, Stateline, Nev. (Retained NABF Heavyweight Title)	KO	8

1973

Feb. 14	Joe Bugner, Las Vegas	W	12
Mar. 31	Ken Norton, San Diego (Lost NABF Heavyweight Title)	L	12
Sept. 10	Ken Norton, Los Angeles (Regained NABF Heavyweight Title)	W	12
Oct. 20	Rudi Lubbers, Jakarta	W	12

1974

Jan. 20	Joe Frazier, New York (Retained NABF Heavyweight Title)	W	12
Oct. 30	George Foreman, Kinshasa, Zaïre, (Regained World Heavyweight Title)	KO	8

1975

Mar. 24	Chuck Wepner, Cleveland (Retained World Heavyweight Title)	KO	15
May 16	Ron Lyle, Las Vegas (Retained World Heavyweight Title)	KO	11
July 1	Joe Bugner, Kuala Lumpur (Retained World Heavyweight Title)	W	15
Oct. 1	Joe Frazier, Manila (Retained World Heavyweight Title)	KO	14

1976

Feb. 20	Jean Pierre Coopman, San Juan (Retained World Heavyweight Title)	KO	5
Apr. 30	Jimmy Young, Landover (Retained World Heavyweight Title)	W	15
May 24	Richard Dunn, Munich (Retained World Heavyweight Title)	KO	5
June 25	Antonio Inoki, Tokyo (Above match was a boxer against a wrestler)	Exh. D	15
Sept. 28	Ken Norton, New York (Retained World Heavyweight Title)	W	15

1977

Jan. 29	Peter Fuller, Boston	Exh.	4
Jan. 29	Walter Haines, Boston	Exh.	1
Jan. 29	Jeyy Houston, Boston	Exh.	2
Jan. 29	Ron Drinkwater, Boston	Exh.	2
Jan. 29	Matt Ross, Boston	Exh.	2
Jan. 29	Frank Smith, Boston	Exh.	1
May 16	Alfredo Evangelista, Landover (Retained World Heavyweight Title)	W	15
Sept. 29	Earnie Shavers, New York (Retained World Heavyweight Title)	W	15
Dec. 2	Scott Le Doux, Chicago	Exh.	5

1978

Feb. 15	Leon Spinks, Las Vegas (Lost World Heavyweight Title)	L	15
Sept. 15	Leon Spinks, New Orleans (Regained World Heavyweight Title)	W	15

Roberto Duran and Leonard, November 1980

1979

Announced retirement

1980

Oct. 2	Larry Holmes, Las Vegas (For World Heavyweight Title)	KO by	11

1981

Dec. 11	Trevor Berbick, Nassau	L	10

TB	KO	WD	WF	D	LD	LF	KO BY	ND	NC
61	37	19	0	0	4	0	1	0	0

ROBERTO DURAN

Born, June 16, 1951, Guarare, Panama. Weight, 114–155 lbs. Height, 5 ft 7 in. Managed by Carlos Eleta.

1967

Mar. 8	Carlos Mendoza, Colon	W	4
Apr. 4	Manuel Jimenez, Colon	KO	1
May 14	Juan Gondola, Colon	KO	1
May 30	Eduardo Morales, Panama City	KO	1
Aug. 10	Enrique Jacobo, Panama City	KO	1

1968

June 20	Eduardo Morales, Panama City	KO	1
Aug. 25	Leroy Cargill, Panama City	KO	1
Sept. 22	Cesar de Leon, Panama City	KO	1
Dec. 7	Carlos Howard, Panama City	KO	1

1969

Jan. 19	Alberto Brand, Panama City	KO	4
Feb. 1	Eduardo Fruto, Panama City	W	8
May 18	Jacinto Garcia, Panama City	KO	4
June 22	Adolfo Osses, Panama City	KO	7
July 16	Serafin Garcia, Panama City	KO	5
Nov. 23	Luis Patino, Panama City	KO	8

1970

Apr. 5	Felipe Torres, Mexico City	W	10
May 16	Ernesto Marcel, Panama City	KO	10
July 10	Clemente Mucino, Colon	KOI	6
Sept. 5	Marvin Castanedas, Puerto Armuelles	KO	1

1971

Jan. 10	Nacho Castanedas, Panama City	KO	4
Mar. 5	Jose Angel Herrera, Mexico City	KO	6
Apr. 4	Jose Acosta, Panama City	KO	1
May 29	Lloyd Marshall, Panama City	KO	6
July 18	Fermin Soto, Monterrey	KO	3
Sept. 13	Benny Huertas, New York	KO	1
Oct. 1	Hiroshi Kobayashi, Panama City	KO	7

1972

Jan. 15	Angel Robinson Garcia, Panama City	W	10
Mar. 10	Francisco Munoz, Panama City	KO	1
June 26	Ken Buchanan, New York (Won World Lightweight Title)	Ko	13
Sept. 2	Greg Potter, Panama City	KO	1
Oct. 29	Lupe Ramirez, Panama City	KO	1

Marvin Hagler and John Mugabi, March 1986

Nov. 17	Esteban DeJesus, New York	L	10
1973			
Jan. 20	Jimmy Robertson, Panama City	KO	5
	(Retained World Lightweight Title)		
Feb. 23	Juan Medina, Los Angeles	KO	7
Mar. 17	Javier Ayala, Los Angeles	W	10
Apr. 14	Gerado Ferrat, Panama City	KO	2
June 2	Hector Thompson, Panama City	KO	8
	(Retained World Lightweight Title)		
Aug. 4	Doc McClendon, San Juan	W	10
Sept. 8	Ishimatsu Suzuki, Panama City	KO	10
	(Retained World Lightweight Title)		
Dec. 1	Tony Garcia, Santiago	KO	2
1974			
Jan. 21	Leonard Tavarez, Paris	KO	4
Feb. 16	Armando Mendoza, Panama City	KO	3
Mar. 16	Esteban DeJesus, Panama City	KO	11
	(Retained World Lightweight Title)		
July 6	Flash Gallego, Panama City	KO	5
Sept. 2	Hector Matta, San Juan	W	10
Oct. 31	Jose Vasquez, San Jose	KO	2
Nov. 16	Adelberto Vanegas, Panama City	KO	1
Dec. 21	Masataka Takayama, San Jose	KO	1
	(Retained World Lightweight Title)		
1975			
Feb. 15	Andres Salgado, Panama City	KO	1
Mar. 2	Ray Lampkin, Panama City	KO	14
	(Retained World Lightweight Title)		
June 3	Jose Peterson, Miami Beach	KO	1
Aug. 2	Pedro Mendoza, Managua	KO	1
Sept. 13	Alirio Acuna, Chitre	KO	3
Sept. 30	Edwin Viruet, Uniondale	W	10
Dec. 14	Leonico Ortiz, San Juan	KO	15
	(Retained World Lightweight Title)		
1976			
May 4	Saoul Mamby, Miami Beach	W	10
May 22	Lou Bizzarro, Erie	KO	14
	(Retained World Lightweight Title)		
July 31	Emiliano Villa, Panama City	KO	9
Oct. 15	Alvaro Rojas, Hollywood, Fla	KO	1
	(Retained World Lightweight Title)		
1977			
Jan. 29	Vilomar Fernandez, Miami Beach	KO	13
	(Retained World Lightweight Title)		
May 16	Javier Muniz, Landover	W	10
Aug. 6	Bernandro Diaz, Panama City	KO	1
Sept. 17	Edwin Viruet, Philadelphia	W	15
	(Retained World Lightweight Title)		
1978			
Jan 21	Esteban DeJesus, Las Vegas	KO	12
	(Retained World Lightweight Title)		
Apr. 27	Adolph Viruet, New York	W	10
Sept. 1	Ezequiel Obando, Panama City	KO	2
Dec. 8	Monroe Brooks, New York	KO	8
1979			
Feb. 1	Relinquished World Lightweight Title.		
Apr. 8	Jimmy Heair, Las Vegas	W	10
June 22	Carlos Palomino, New York	W	10
Sept. 28	Zeferino Gonzalez, Las Vegas	W	10
1980			
Jan. 13	Josef Nsubuga, Las Vegas	KO	4
Feb. 24	Wellington Wheatley, Las Vegas	KO	6
June 20	Ray Leonard, Montreal	W	15
	(Won World Welterweight Title)		
Nov. 25	Ray Leonard, New Orleans	KO by	8
	(Lost World Welterweight Title)		
1981			
June 10	Simon Smith, New York	Exh.	3
Aug. 9	Nino Gonzalez, Cleveland	W	10
Sept. 26	Luigi Minchillo, Las Vegas	W	10
1982			
Jan. 30	Wilfred Benitez, Las Vegas	L	15
	(For WBC Junior Middleweight Title)		
Sept 4	Kirkland Laing, Detroit	L	10
Nov. 12	Jimmy Batten, Miami, Fla	W	10
1983			
Jan. 29	Pipino Cuevas, Los Angeles	W	4
June 16	Davey Moore, New York	W	9
	(WBA Light Middleweight Title)		
Nov. 10	Marvin Hagler, Las Vegas	L	15
	(World Middleweight Title Challenge)		
June 16	Thomas Hearns, Las Vegas	W	2
	(World Middleweight Title Challenge)		
1986			
Jan. 31	Manuel Zambrano, Panama	W	2
Apr. 18	Jorge Suero, Panama	W	2
June 23	Robbie Sims, Las Vegas	L	10
1987			
May 16	Victor Claudio, Miami	W	10
Sept 12	Juan C. Giminez, Miami	W	10
1988			
Feb. 5	Ricky Stackhouse, Atlantic City	W	10
Apr. 14	Paul Thorn, Atlantic City	W	6
Nov. 1	Jeff Tomas, Chicago	W	10
1989			
Feb. 24	Iran Barkley, Atlantic City	W	12
	(Won WBC Middleweight Title).		
Dec. 9	Sugar Ray Leonard, Las Vegas.	L	12
	(WBC super-middleweight title challenge).		

KO	TB	WD	WF	D	LD	LF	KO BY	ND	NC
56	80	19	0	0	4	0	1	0	0

MARVIN HAGLER

Born, May 23, 1954, Newark, N.J. Weight, 158 lbs. Height, 5ft 9 1/2 in. Southpaw. Managed by Goody and Pat Petronelli.

1973 National AAU Middleweight Champion

1973			
May 18	Terry Ryan, Brockton	KO	2

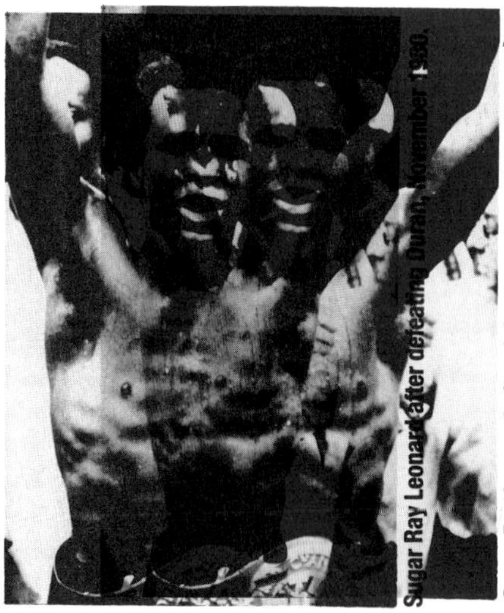

Sugar Ray Leonard after defeating Duran, November 1980.

Sugar Ray Leonard after defeating Duran, November 1980.

Date	Opponent, Place	Result	Rounds
July 25	Sonny Williams, Boston	W	6
Aug. 8	Muhammad Smith, Boston	KO	2
Oct. 6	Don Wigfall, Brockton	W	8
Oct. 26	Cove Green, Brockton	KO	4
Nov. 18	Cocoa Kid, Brockton	KO	2
Dec. 17	Manny Freitas, Portland, Me	KO	1
Dec. 18	James Redford, Boston	KO	4
1974			
Feb. 5	Bob Harrington, Boston	KO	5
Apr. 5	Tracy Morrison, Boston	KO	8
May 4	Jim Redford, Brockton	KO	2
May 30	Curtis Phillips, Portland	KO	5
July 16	Robert Williams, Boston	KO	3
Aug. 13	Peachy Davis, New Bedford	KO	1
Aug. 30	Ray Seales, Boston	W	10
Oct. 29	Morris Jordan, New Bedford	KO	4
Nov. 16	George Green, Brockton	KO	1
Nov. 26	Ray Seales, Seattle	D	10
Dec. 20	D.C. Walker, Boston	KO	2
1975			
Feb. 15	Don Wigfall, Brockton	KO	5
Mar. 31	Joey Blair, Boston	KO	2
Apr. 14	Jimmy Owens, Boston	W	10
May 24	Jimmy Owens, Brockton	W disq.	6
Aug. 7	Jesse Bender, Portland	KO	1
Sept. 30	Lamont Lovelady, Boston	KO	7
Dec. 20	Johnny Baldwin, Boston	W	10
1976			
Jan. 13	Bobby Watts, Philadelphia	L	10
Feb. 7	Matt Donovan, Boston	KO	2
Mar. 9	Willie Monroe, Philadelphia	L	10
June 2	Bob Smith, Taunton	KO	5
Aug. 3	D.C. Walker, Providence	KO	6
Sept. 14	Eugene Hart, Philadelphia	KO	8
Dec. 21	George Davis, Boston	KO	6
1977			
Feb. 15	Willie Monroe, Boston	KO	12
Mar. 16	Reginald Ford, Boston	KO	3
June 10	Roy Jones, Hartford	KO	3
Aug. 23	Willie Monroe, Philadelphia	KO	2
Sept. 24	Ray Philips, Boston	KO	7
Oct. 15	Jim Henry, Providence	W	10
Nov. 26	Mike Colbert, Boston	KO	12
1978			
Mar. 4	Kevin Finnegan, Boston	KO	9
Apr. 7	Doug Demmings, Los Angeles	KO	8
May 13	Kevin Finnegan, Boston	KO	7
Aug. 24	Bennie Briscoe, Philadelphia	W	10
Nov. 11	Willie Warren, Boston	KO	7
1979			
Feb. 3	Ray Seales, Boston	KO	1
Mar. 12	Bob Patterson, Providence	KO	3
May 26	Jaime Thomas, Portland, Me.	KO	3
June 30	Norberto Cabrera, Monte Carlo	KO	8
Nov. 30	Vito Antuofermo, Las Vegas (For World Middleweight Title)	D	15
1980			
Feb. 16	Loucif Hamani, Portland	KO	2
Apr. 19	Bobby Watts, Portland	KO	2
May 17	Marcos Geraldo, Las Vegas	W	10
Sept. 27	Alan Minter, London (Won World Middleweight Title)	KO	3
1981			
Jan. 17	Fulgencio Obelmejias, Boston (Retained World Middleweight Title)	KO	8
June 13	Vito Antuofermo, Boston (Retained World Middleweight Title)	KO	5
Oct. 3	Mustafa Hamsho, Rosemont (Retained World Middleweight Title)	KO	11
1982			
Mar. 7	Wm. (Caveman) Lee, Atlantic City (Retained World Middleweight Title)	KO	1
Oct. 30	Fulgencio Obelmejias, San Remo, Italy (Defence of the World Middleweight Title)	W	5
1983			
Feb. 11	Tony Sibson, Worcester USA (Defence of the World Middleweight Title)	W	5
May 27	Wilford Scypion, Providence, USA (Defence of the World Middleweight Title)	W	4
Nov. 10	Roberto Duran, Las Vegas (Defence of the World Middleweight Title)	W	15
1984			
Mar. 30	Juan Domingo Roldan, Las Vegas (Defence of the World Middleweight Title)	W	10
Oct. 19	Mustafa Hamsho, New York (Defence of the World Middleweight Title)	W	3
1985			
Apr. 16	Thomas Hearns, Las Vegas (Defence of the World Middleweight Title)	W	3
1986			
Mar. 10	John Mugabi, Las Vegas (Defence of the World Middleweight Title)	W	11
1987			
Apr. 6	Sugar Ray Leonard, Las Vegas (Defence of the World Middleweight Title)	L	12

TB	KO	WD	WF	D	LD	LF	KO BY	ND	NC
73	41	22	0	2	7	0	1	0	0

SUGAR RAY LEONARD

Date	Opponent, Place	Result	Rounds
1977			
Feb. 5	Luis Vega, Baltimore	W	6
May 14	Willie Rodriguez, Baltimore	W	6
June 10	Vinnie DeBarros, Hartford	KO	3
Sept. 24	Frank Santore, Baltimore	KO	5
Nov. 5	Augustin Estrada, Las Vegas	KO	5
Dec. 17	Hector Diaz, Washington, D.C.	KO	2

RECORDS

Date	Opponent	Result	Rounds
1978			
Feb. 4	Rocky Ramon, Baltimore	W	8
Mar. 1	Art McKnight, Dayton	KO	7
Mar. 19	Javier Muniz, New Haven,	KO	1
Apr. 13	Bobby Haymon, Landover,	KO	3
May. 13	Randy Milton, Utica	KO	8
June 3	Rafael Rodriquez, Baltimore	W	10
July 18	Dick Ecklund, Boston	W	10
Sept. 9	Floyd Mayweather, Providence	KO	9
Oct. 6	Randy Shields, Baltimore	W	10
Nov. 3	Bernardo Prada, Portland, ME	W	10
Dec. 9	Armando Muniz, Springfield, Mass	KO	6
1979			
Jan. 11	Johnny Gant, Landover	KO	8
Feb. 11	Fernando Marcotte, Miami Beach	KO	8
Mar. 24	Daniel Gonzales, Tucson	KO	1
Apr. 21	Adolfo Viruet, Las Vegas	W	10
May 20	Marcos Geraldo, New Orleans	W	10
June 24	Tony Chiaverini, Las Vegas	KO	4
Aug. 12	Peter Ranzany, Las Vegas (Won NABF Welterweight Title)	KO	4
Sept. 28	Andy Price, Las Vegas (Retained NABF Welterweight Title)	KO	1
Nov. 30	Wilfred Benitez, Las Vegas (Won WBC Welterweight Title)	KO	15
1980			
Mar. 31	Dave (Boy) Green, Landover (Retained WBC Welterweight Title)	KO	4
June 20	Roberto Duran, Montreal (Lost WBC Welterweight Title)	L	15
Nov. 25	Roberto Duran, New Orleans (Regained WBC Welterweight Title)	KO	8
1981			
Mar. 28	Larry Bonds, Syracuse (Retained WBC Welterweight Title)	KO	10
Jun. 25	Ayub Kalule, Houston (Won WBA Junior Middleweight Title)	KO	9
Sep. 16	Thomas Hearns, Las Vegas (Won undisputed World Welterweight Title)	KO	14
1982			
Feb. 15	Bruce Finch, Reno (Retained undisputed World Welterweight Title)	KO	3
Nov. 9	Announced retirement		
1983			
(Inactive)			
1984			
May 11	Kevin Howard, Worcester	KO	9
1985			
(Inactive)			
1986			
(Inactive)			
1987			
Apr. 6	Marvelous Marvin Hagler, Las Vegas (Won WBC middleweight title)	W	12
1988			
Nov. 7	Donny Lalonde, Las Vegas (Won WBC super middleweight and light heavyweight titles)	KO	9
1989			
June 12	Thomas Hearns Draw 12 Las Vegas		
Dec. 9	Roberto Duran, Las Vegas. (Retained WBC super-middleweight title)	W	12

Career Record

Total Bouts	Won	(KOs)	Lost	Drew
38	36	25	1	1

Mighty Mike Tyson

MIKE TYSON

Date	Opponent	Result	Rounds
1985			
Mar. 6	Hector Merced, Albany	KO	1
Apr. 190	Trent Singleton, Albany	KO	1
May 23	Donald Halpin, Albany	KO	4
June 20	Rick Spain, Atlantic City	KO	1
July 11	John Alderson, Altantic City	KO	3
July 19	Larry Sims, Poughkeepsie	KO	1
Aug. 15	Lorenzo Canady, Atlantic City	KO	1
Sept. 5	Michael Johnson, Atlantic City	KO	1
Oct. 9	Donnie Long, Atlantic City	KO	1
Oct. 25	Robert Colay, Atlantic City	KO	1
Nov. 1	Sterling Benjamin, Latham	KO	1
Nov. 13	Eddie Richardson, Houston	KO	1
Nov. 22	Conroy Nelson, Albany	KO	2
Dec. 6	Sam Scaff, New York	KO	1
Dec. 27	Mark Young, Colonie	KO	1
1986			
Jan. 11	David Jaco, Albany	KO	1
Jan. 24	Mike Jameson, Atlantic City	KO	5
Feb. 16	Jesse Ferguson, Troy	KO	6
Mar. 10	Steve Zouski, Uniondale	KO	3
May 3	James "Quick" Tillis, New York	W	10
May 20	Mitch Green, New York	W	10
June 13	Reggie Gross, New York	KO	1
June 28	William Hosea, Troy	KO	1
July 11	Lorenzo Boyd, Stevensville	KO	2
July 26	Marvis Frazier, Atlantic City	KO	1
Aug. 17	Jose Ribalta, Atlantic City	KO	10
Sept. 6	Alfonso Ratliff, Las Vegas	KO	2
Nov. 22	Trevor Berbick, Las Vegas (Won WBC Heavyweight Championship)	KO	2
1987			
Mar. 7	James Smith, Las Vegas (Won WBA–WBC Heavyweight Championship)	W	12
May 30	Pinklon Thomas, Las Vegas (Retained WBA–WBC Heavyweight Championship)	KO	6
Aug. 1	Tony Tucker, Las Vegas (Won undisputed World Heavyweight Championship)	W	12
Oct. 16	Tyrell Biggs, Atlantic City (Retained undisputed Heavyweight Championship)	KO	7
Jan. 22	Larry Holmes, Atlantic City, (WBA and WBC Heavyweight Title Defence)	W	4
Mar. 21	Tony Tubbs, Tokyo (World Heavyweight Title)	W	2
1989			
Jan. 27	Michael Spinks, Atlantic City, (World Heavyweight Title defence)	KO	1
Feb. 25	Frank Bruno, Las Vegas (World Heavyweight Title defence)	W	5
July 21	Carl Williams, Atlantic City. (Undisputed Heavyweight Championship defence)	KO	1
1990			
Feb. 12	James Douglas (Lost undisputed Heavyweight Championship)	KO by	10

33–1; 29 KOs